Starting Points for Yo[ur]
Internet Exploration

The Web is like thousands of TV channels, or 10,000 New York Public Libraries—it includes volumes and volumes of information. You can browse the Web, following links in an intuitive way, or you can search for what interests you. Here is a brief list of good starting places. Each of these documents lists or organizes other documents to make it easy for you to find your way to the documents you find intriguing or useful.

Yahoo List of Internet Resources

    http://www.yahoo.com

University of Illinois at Urbana-Champaign Index to Web Pages

    http://www.cen.uiuc.edu/~jj9544/index.html

The InterNIC (Network Information Center)

    http://www.internic.net/infoguide.html

The Virtual Reference Desk from UC Irvine

    gopher://peg.cwis.uci.edu:7000/11/gopher.
    welcome/peg/uci

The Clearinghouse for Subject-Oriented Internet Resource Guides

    http://http2.sils.umich.edu/~lou/chhome.html

Scott Yanoff's list of Internet Resources

    http://slacvx.slac.stanford.edu/misc/
    internet-services.html

NCSA Mosaic World Wide Web Starting Points Document

    http://www.ncsa.uiuc.edu/SDG/Software/Mosaic/
    StartingPoints/NetworkStartingPoints.html

The NCSA Mosaic What's New Page

    http://www.ncsa.uiuc.edu/SDG/Software/Mosaic/Docs/
    whats-new.html

FOR EVERY COMPUTER QUESTION,
THERE IS A SYBEX BOOK THAT HAS THE ANSWER

Each computer user learns in a different way. Some need thorough, methodical explanations, while others are too busy for details. At Sybex we bring nearly 20 years of experience to developing the book that's right for you. Whatever your needs, we can help you get the most from your software and hardware, at a pace that's comfortable for you.

We start beginners out right. You will learn by seeing and doing with our **Quick & Easy** series: friendly, colorful guidebooks with screen-by-screen illustrations. For hardware novices, the **Your First** series offers valuable purchasing advice and installation support.

Often recognized for excellence in national book reviews, our **Mastering** titles are designed for the intermediate to advanced user, without leaving the beginner behind. A **Mastering** book provides the most detailed reference available. Add our pocket-sized **Instant Reference** titles for a complete guidance system. Programmers will find that the new **Developer's Handbook** series provides a more advanced perspective on developing innovative and original code.

With the breathtaking advances common in computing today comes an ever increasing demand to remain technologically up-to-date. In many of our books, we provide the added value of software, on disks or CDs. Sybex remains your source for information on software development, operating systems, networking, and every kind of desktop application. We even have books for kids. Sybex can help smooth your travels on the **Internet** and provide **Strategies and Secrets** to your favorite computer games.

As you read this book, take note of its quality. Sybex publishes books written by experts—authors chosen for their extensive topical knowledge. In fact, many are professionals working in the computer software field. In addition, each manuscript is thoroughly reviewed by our technical, editorial, and production personnel for accuracy and ease-of-use before you ever see it—our guarantee that you'll buy a quality Sybex book every time.

To manage your hardware headaches and optimize your software potential, ask for a Sybex book.

FOR MORE INFORMATION, PLEASE CONTACT:

Sybex Inc.
2021 Challenger Drive
Alameda, CA 94501
Tel: (510) 523-8233 • (800) 227-2346
Fax: (510) 523-2373

SYBEX

Sybex is committed to using natural resources wisely to preserve and improve our environment. As a leader in the computer books publishing industry, we are aware that over 40% of America's solid waste is paper. This is why we have been printing our books on recycled paper since 1982.

This year our use of recycled paper will result in the saving of more than 153,000 trees. We will lower air pollution effluents by 54,000 pounds, save 6,300,000 gallons of water, and reduce landfill by 27,000 cubic yards.

In choosing a Sybex book you are not only making a choice for the best in skills and information, you are also choosing to enhance the quality of life for all of us.

Let us hear from you.

 Talk to SYBEX authors, editors and fellow forum members.

 Get tips, hints and advice online.

 Download magazine articles, book art, and shareware.

Join the SYBEX Forum on CompuServe®

If you're already a CompuServe user, just type **GO SYBEX** to join the SYBEX Forum. If not, try CompuServe for free by calling 1-800-848-8199 and ask for Representative 560. You'll get one free month of basic service and a $15 credit for CompuServe extended services—a $23.95 value. Your personal ID number and password will be activated when you sign up.

SYBEX

Join us online today. Type **GO SYBEX** on CompuServe. If you're not a CompuServe member, call Representative 560 at **1-800-848-8199**.

(outside U.S./Canada call 614-457-0802)

Daniel A. Tauber and Brenda Kienan

SYBEX®

San Francisco • Paris • Düsseldorf • Soest

Acquisitions Editor: Kristine Plachy
Developmental Editor: Steve Lipson
Editor: Vivian Perry
Project Editor: Malcolm Faulds
Technical Editor: Aaron Kushner
Chapter Artist: Lucka Zivny
Desktop Publisher: Lynell Decker
Production Assistant: Kate Westrich
Indexer: Ted Laux
Cover Designer: Joanna Kim Gladden

Library of Congress Card Number: 94-74149

ISBN: 0-7821-1656-6

Manufactured in the United States of America

10 9 8 7 6 5

To Robert & Halley Maclean Boyer and Harry & Adele Tauber

—pioneers all

Acknowledgments

The book you hold in your hands is the result of a truly collaborative effort; we are indebted to the many people who helped to make it a reality.

At Spry, thanks to David Pool, Kevin Britt, and Lisa Thorell, as well as the team that developed Air Mosaic, a wonderful product.

At Sybex, our thanks go to Dr. R.S. Langer and to Steve Lipson, who brought us to this surprising project; also to Vivian Perry and Malcolm Faulds, possibly the world's most patient and persistent editing team; and to Aaron Kushner, who stood at the ready and then flew through the manuscript.

Special thanks to Barbara Gordon, Chris Meredith, Carrie Lavine, Kristine Plachy, Janet Boone, and Celeste Grinage, the unsung heroines of Sybex.

Many thanks are owed to the production team of Lynell Decker and Kate Westrich, who picked up the ball several times over; to Lucka Zivny, who created the charming line drawings; to indexer Ted Laux, who compiled references with admirable compulsion; to assistant editors Stephanie La Croix and Emily Smith, without whom nothing would ever get into production; and to cover designer Joanna Gladden, who outdoes herself again and again.

Thanks go to Kelli Wiseth and Joe Sciallo, who researched and drafted the early chapters. Thanks also to Nancy Stokesberry at Practical Peripherals for arranging the loan of a modem.

Our gratitude goes as always to family and friends for their continued support and all the understanding they can muster. Special thanks to:

◆ Margaret Tauber, Ron and Frances Tauber, Jessica and Martin Grant, and the rest of the Tauber family; also to Gino Reynoso.

◆ Joani Buerhle, Sharon Crawford, Jerry Doty, Rion Dugan, Thaisa Frank, Fred Frumberg, Carol Heller, Karen Kevorkian, Kathleen Lattinville, Xuan Mai Le, the McArdle family, Amy Miller, Carolyn Miller, Lonnie Moseley, Mrs. W. Moseley and her family, Freeman Ng, Ron Nyren, Carol Piasanti, Cordell Sloan, John Undercoffer, Mary Undercoffer, the Undercoffer brothers, Savitha Varadan, Sally Borie Wilson, and Robert E. Williams III.

Contents at a Glance

Contents

Part Two: Using Air Mosaic
50

Chapter 3:

Running Air Mosaic
51

Chapter 4:

Good and Useful Starting Points

79

Chapter 5:

Spots on the Web You Won't Want to Miss

99

Chapter 6:

Tools and Techniques for Searching and Finding

139

Part Three: Beyond the Basics
158

Chapter 7:

You Too Can Be a Web Publisher

159

Chapter 8:

Getting and Installing Video Viewers and Sound Players

195

Appendix:

Installing and Setting Up the Software
217

Glossary
233

Index
243

Introduction

Everybody wants to get on the Internet. If you want to join in the action but you don't want to learn Unix and type a lot of archaic commands to get anywhere, read on. This book, written in plain English and filled with how-to know-how, is a complete solution that will get you started in no time exploring and using the World Wide Web, the fastest growing part of the Internet.

What's on the Disk

On the disk that comes with this book, you'll find a licensed copy of Spry Mosaic, an instant Internet access product that is the functional equivalent of Mosaic in a Box (available in software retail outlets). Spry Mosaic, which has all the features of Mosaic in a Box, includes on one disk:

◆ Spry's Air Mosaic, the acclaimed Web browser that PC Magazine has named a "Best Product of the Year"

◆ Instant Internet access via CompuServe's specialized network with over 400 points of presence (local phone numbers)

◆ SLIP/PPP software that is preconfigured to work with Air Mosaic and the special CompuServe Internet access service

All this software is *preconfigured*—it's set up to work together so smoothly you won't even know it's there. All you'll ever see on your screen is Air Mosaic, working like a charm.

The account you'll be setting up with CompuServe so you can use this product is specially designed to give you access to the Internet's World Wide Web via Spry's Air Mosaic. Installation instructions are in the appendix.

If You Need Help

Technical support is available from Spry at (206) 447-0958 Monday through Friday between 8 a.m. and 5 p.m. (Pacific standard time). For general information or billing questions, you can call Spry at (206) 447-0300, also during business hours, or at (800) SPRYNET. Spry's URL is `http://www.spry.com`.

There are other Mosaics available (you've probably heard of them), but most forms of Mosaic require that you have an Internet service provider, download Mosaic, install SLIP/PPP software so you can make your Mosaic connection, and then *configure all this stuff* so it will work together. What's more, every time you start your Web explorations with most Mosaics, you'll have to start your service provider, then start SLIP/PPP, and only then can you start up Mosaic.

Air Mosaic is truly a plug-and-play product that does all the work for you. It installs itself in minutes, and starts up in seconds, taking you straight onto the best, most vital part of the Internet, the World Wide Web.

Is This Book for You?

If you want to start exploring the World Wide Web using an easy-to-install, easy-to-start-up, powerful Web browser, Spry Mosaic is for you, and if Spry's product is for you, so is this book.

This book was written by two Internauts with years of combined experience. It's written in plain English, avoiding jargon and explaining any necessary terms clearly. It's a great start for beginners, but that's not all—because it includes complete information on publishing on the Internet and on getting and using special tools to enhance your Web experience, this book is a good follow-up for people who already have some Internet experience.

How This Book Is Organized

This book is organized into eight chapters, beginning, logically enough, with Chapter 1, a brief introduction to the Internet. Chapter 2 goes into more detail about the World Wide Web, and how the software that comes with this book can get you there. Chapter 3 tells you in basic terms how to use the product, Chapter 4 describes some good jumping off places for your Web travels, and Chapter 5 describes some good and useful places you might want to visit. With basic navigation skills under your belt, you might want to focus your Web travels, so Chapter 6 tells you how to use Air Mosaic's search capabilities. Chapter 7 follows up by showing you how you, too, can be a Web publisher—it includes a primer on HTML, the mark-up language used to create Web documents, along with tips for successful Web page design and information on how to publicize your Web page. Chapter 8 tells you how to get and use sound players and video viewers—special tools that will further enhance your experience of Air Mosaic and the World Wide Web.

Internet and Web terms are defined throughout the book, but you might want to look up something as you go along, so toward the back of the book you'll find a handy glossary.

Spry Mosaic is easy to install; there are a few things to know, however, so you'll find complete installation instructions in the appendix.

Conventions Used in This Book

Mosaic Access to the Internet uses various conventions to help you find the information you need quickly and effortlessly. Tips, Notes, and Warnings, shown here, are placed strategically throughout the book, to help you home in on important information in a snap.

Here you'll find insider tips and shortcuts—information meant to help you use Air Mosaic more adeptly.

Here you'll find reminders, asides, and bits of important information that should be emphasized.

 Here you'll find cautionary information describing trouble spots you may encounter either in using the software or in using the Internet.

A simple kind of shorthand used in this book helps to save space so more crucial matters can be discussed; in this system, directions to "pull down the File menu and select Save" will appear as "select File ➤ Save," and the phrase "press Enter" appears as "press ↵," for example—again, these conventions are described as they are introduced.

Long (but important or interesting) digressions are set aside as boxed text, called *sidebars*.

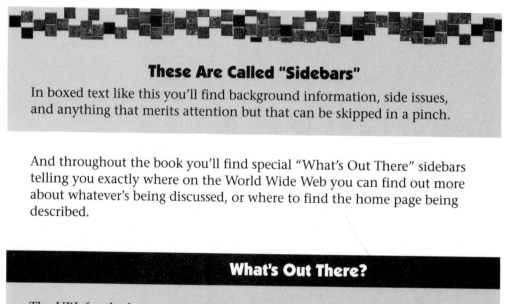

These Are Called "Sidebars"

In boxed text like this you'll find background information, side issues, and anything that merits attention but that can be skipped in a pinch.

And throughout the book you'll find special "What's Out There" sidebars telling you exactly where on the World Wide Web you can find out more about whatever's being discussed, or where to find the home page being described.

What's Out There?

The URL for the home page of interest at the moment will appear in a different font, like http://cuiwww.unige.ch/w3catalog.

The Sybex Home Page

If you want to find out more about what Sybex has to offer in the way of Internet-related books, check out the Sybex home page at http://www.sybex.com. There you'll find access to an online version of the Sybex catalog, announcements of upcoming books, and information about special promotions.

Let's Get This Show on the Road...

Enough about what's in the book and on the disk—to start your Internet exploration, turn to Chapter 1; to find out how to install the software, turn to the appendix.

Part One:

The Internet,
the World Wide Web, and Mosaic

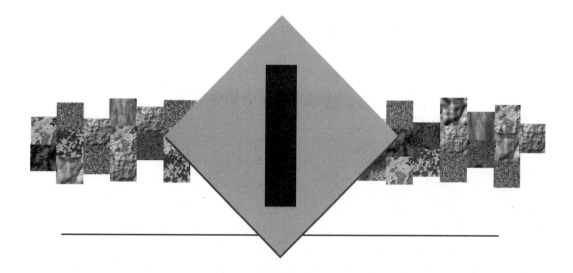

The Big Picture

You'd have to live in a vacuum these days not to have heard of the Internet. Scarcely a day goes by without some mention of it on the nightly news or in the local paper, and Internet e-mail addresses are even becoming common in advertisements and on business cards. Millions of people—inspired by excited talk and armed with spanking new accounts with Internet service providers—are taking to the Internet, with visions of adventures on the "information superhighway."

Contrary to all the fashionable hype, the first time you attempt to "cruise" the Internet, you may be in for a rude awakening. Until recently, most access to the Internet was via text-based viewers that left a lot to be desired in the realm of aesthetics and ease of use. The Internet was trafficked for a long time only by academicians and almost nerdly computer enthusiasts.

In fact, with your old or low-budget Internet account a prompt that looks like this:

%

may be all you get, even if you're running the thing under Windows. Your trek into cyberspace may feel more like a bumpy ride on an old bicycle.

● An Air Mosaic View of the Internet

That's why Air Mosaic is so great: it offers an elegant point-and-click interface to guide you through the Internet's coolest resources, all linked to a growing number of global Internet resources. Air Mosaic is a *browser*—a program with which you can view graphically intriguing, linked documents all over the world and search and access information in a few quick mouse-clicks. You don't have to type cryptic commands or deal with screens filled with plain text; all you have to do is point and click on highlighted words (or pictures) to follow the links between related information in a single, giant web of linked "pages." Figure 1.1 compares a text-based view of the Internet to an Air Mosaic view.

 Mosaic was originally distributed free of charge over the Internet itself. Later, its developers licensed the rights to distribute Mosaic to a number of companies who enhanced the product and sold it commercially. This book includes with it Spry's Air Mosaic, in a package that installs itself and gets you on the Internet in seconds.

Within the Internet is a special network of linked documents known as the World Wide Web. With Air Mosaic, you can perform point-and-click online research on the Web or just follow your whims along an intuitive path of discovery. Air Mosaic is a Windows-based product, so a lot of the tasks you do in other Windows programs (like Save) work in ways already familiar to you.

To run most forms of Mosaic on your PC, you need a dial-up connection to the Internet via a service provider, and not just any service provider—you need one with specific capabilities. You also need software (known as SLIP or PPP) that provides a connection between Mosaic and your Internet service provider. Don't worry, this is not necessary with the software that came with this book.

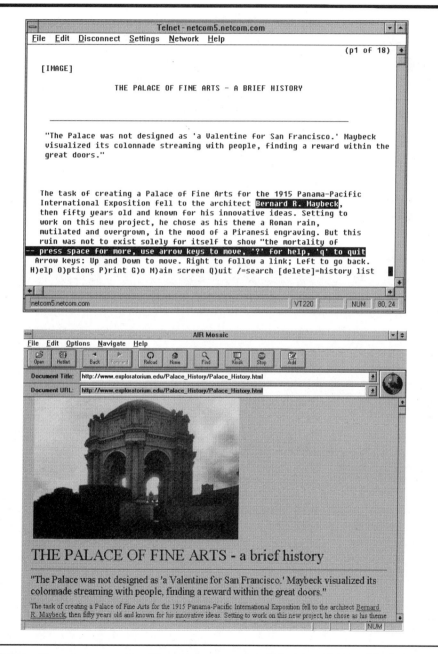

FIGURE 1.1: Here you can see the difference between the old text-based view of the Internet (top) and the easy-to-use, graphically pleasing Air Mosaic view of the Internet (bottom).

Spry Mosaic, the product that comes with this book, includes Air Mosaic (an enhanced form of the popular Web browser), SLIP/PPP connection software, and even Internet service (through CompuServe's specialized network)—all preconfigured to work together seamlessly. No downloading, no configuring, no starting up the connecting software before you start Air Mosaic. It just works.

Let's take a quick look at the Internet. Then, in the next chapter, we'll investigate how the Web fits into the Internet and just what kinds of stuff you can look at out there using Spry's Air Mosaic.

What's Out There?

As we go along, we're going to tell you what you can find using Air Mosaic and where that stuff is located. You'll see notes like this describing an item of interest and giving you the item's URL (its Uniform Resource Locator or address on the Web). Don't worry if you don't understand this URL business yet—you will soon, and then you can look for the stuff we've described.

What the Internet Is All About

The Internet is a happening thing—interest in the Internet seems to have taken on the proportions of a new national pastime. And yet, when we're asked to define the Internet, many of us are at a loss for words. Even those who are intimately familiar with the "Net" are likely to disagree on a strict definition.

So what is this Internet thing we're hearing so much about? At its most basic level, you can think of the Internet as a vast collection of even vaster libraries of information, all available online for you to look at or to retrieve and use. At another level, the Internet might be thought of as the computers that store the information and the networks that allow you to access the information on the computers. And finally (lest we forget who made the Internet what it is today), it is a collection of *people*—people who act as resources themselves, willing to share their knowledge with the world. This means, of course, that when you interact with the Internet—particularly when you make yourself a resource by sharing communications and information with others—you become a part of the vast network we call the Internet.

The idea of the "information superhighway," popularized in part by the current administration in Washington D.C., is a convenient metaphor: information flowing great distances at incredible speeds, with many on-ramps of access and many potential destinations. In the information superhighway of the future, we might expect an electronic replacement for the everyday postal system (this has already begun to happen in Germany, we're told), and integration of our TV, phone, and newspapers into online information and entertainment services.

What's Out There?

The Electronic Frontier Foundation (EFF) is active in lobbying to ensure that the information superhighway of the future includes protections for individual rights. You can find out about the EFF, and what it is up to, with the URL http://www.eff.org. Other information about the government's initiative for building the information superhighway is available with the URL http://far.mit.edu/diig.html.

We're not quite up to that fully integrated superhighway envisioned by futurists yet, but the Internet as it exists today delivers plenty of power. The resources and information you find on the Internet are available for use on the job, as part of personal or professional research, or for just plain fun. No matter how you view the Internet, the idea that individuals as well as corporations can access information around the world has a particular appeal that borders on the irresistible.

The Internet does act much like a highway system. There are high-speed data paths called *backbones* to connect the major networks; these actually do function much like an electronic version of the interstate highways. There are also lower-speed *links* through which local networks tie in to the Internet, much as city streets feed onto the highway (see Figure 1.2).

The Big Picture

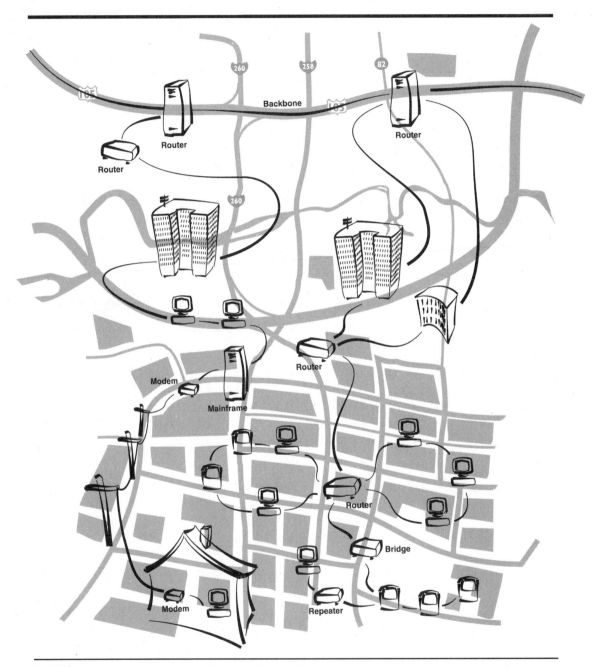

FIGURE 1.2: The Internet can be imagined as a system of highways and roadways, although it doesn't have any real geography.

The beauty of the Internet's system is that not all networks are, or even need to be, directly connected, because the Internet structure is one of *inter-connection*. You can in effect hop from network to network to get where you want and to get what you want.

The highway metaphor begins to break down, however, when you realize that the Internet transcends geography. It's a global system, that's true, but when you use the Net you probably won't be very conscious that the material you're viewing on your screen at one moment is actually located on a machine in Switzerland, and what you see the next moment is actually on a machine in Japan. Perhaps a more accurate metaphor for the Internet would be having a global remote control at your fingertips, able to switch to just about any topic (channel, if you prefer) of your choosing. And now, with user-friendly tools such as Air Mosaic available, access is no longer for just the stereotypical nerd.

Where It All Began

To understand how the Internet came into being, you'd have to go back 30 years or so, to the Cold War era. The think-tank military planners of that age were concerned not only with surviving a nuclear war, but also with communicating in its aftermath if one should occur. They envisioned a control network, linking bases and command posts from state to state, that would remain operational in spite of direct attacks. With this in mind, the U.S. Defense Department's Advanced Research Projects Agency began work on a computer network called ARPAnet during the 1960s.

The principles of the network were simple. It had to operate from the outset as if it were "unreliable"—to adjust up-front for the possibility of downed communication links. Control, therefore, would be decentralized to further minimize any single point of failure. Data would be split up and sent on the network in individual Internet Protocol (IP) *packets*. (A packet can be thought of as similar to an envelope.) Each packet of data would carry within it the address of its destination, and could reach its endpoint by the most efficient route. If part of the network became unavailable, the packets would still be able to get to their destinations and would be reassembled with their full content intact.

Though at first this may sound inefficient, it put the burden of communicating on the computers themselves, rather than on the communications network. That was the foremost issue on the minds of the planners: that the system did not rely on a central *server* (a machine on the network that holds or processes data for the other machines on the network). This proposal linked the computers together as *peers* instead, giving each computer equal status on the network and allowing for different types of computers to communicate, de-emphasizing the communications infrastructure. Thus, even if large pieces of the network were destroyed, the data itself could still reach its destination because it was not concerned with *how* to get there. So it was that the Department of Defense commissioned the initial implementation of ARPAnet in 1969.

Perhaps you work in a business where a lot of machines are cabled together as a LAN (<u>a local area network</u>). Each of these networks is like a smaller version of the Internet, in that a bunch of machines are linked together, but they are not necessarily linked to other networks via phone lines. LANs also usually have a central <u>server</u>—a machine that holds data and processes communications between the linked machines, which is unlike the Internet in that if your LAN server goes down, your network goes down.

Throughout the '70s and early '80s, the ARPAnet continued to grow, and more developments occurred to spur interest in networking and the Internet. Other services and big networks came into being (such as Usenet and Bitnet) and e-mail began to gain wide use as a communications tool. Local area networks (LANs) became increasingly common in business and academic use, and now users no longer wanted to connect just select computers to the Internet but instead were interested in hooking up entire local networks (which might mean all the computers in the organization).

Today the original Internet, the ARPAnet, is no more, having been replaced in 1986 by a new backbone, the National Science Foundation (NSFNet) network. NSFNet forever changed the scope of the Internet in that it permitted more than just a few lucky people in the military, academia, and large corporations to conduct research and access super-computer centers. With all this good, however, came the bad as well: more people using the Internet meant more network traffic, which meant slower response, which meant better connectivity solutions would have to be implemented. Which brings us to where we are today, with demand increasing exponentially as more and more people want to connect to the Internet and discover the online riches of the '90s. (See Figure 1.3.)

Annual rate of growth for World-Wide Web traffic: 341, 634% (1st year)

◆

Annual rate of growth for Gopher traffic: 997%

◆

Number of countries reachable by electronic mail: 159 (approx.)

◆

Number of countries not reachable by electronic mail: 77 (approx.)

◆

Number of countries on the Internet: 81

◆

Average time between new networks connecting to the Internet: 10 minutes

◆

Number of newspaper and magazine articles about the Internet during the first nine
months of 1993: over 2,300

◆

Number of attendees at Internet World, December, 1994: over 10,000
Number of attendees at Internet World, January, 1992: 272

◆

Advertised network numbers in October, 1993: 16,533
Advertised network numbers in October, 1992: 7,505

◆

Date after which more than half the registered networks were commercial: August, 1991

◆

Number of Usenet articles posted in two weeks in December, 1993: 605,000
Number of megabytes of Usenet articles posted: 1,450
Number of users posting Usenet articles: 130,000
Number or Usenet sites represented: 42,000

◆

Number of on-line coffeehouses in San Francisco: 18
Cost for four minutes of Internet time at those coffeehouses: $0.25

◆

Date on which first Stephen King short story published via the Internet before print
publication: 19 September 1993

◆

Round-trip time from Digital CRL to mcmvax.mcmurdo.gov in McMurdo, Antarctica: 640
milliseconds

◆

Amount of time it takes for Supreme Court decisions to become available on the
Internet: less than one day

FIGURE 1.3: These Internet statistics (courtesy of Win Treese) tell an amazing story.

The Burning Questions of Control, Funding, and Use

As odd as it may sound, there is no one person with overall authority for running the Internet. Instead, a group called the Internet Society (ISOC), composed of volunteers, directs the Internet. ISOC appoints a subcouncil, the Internet Architecture Board (IAB), and it is the members of this board who work out issues of standards, network resources, network addresses, and the like. Another volunteer group, the Internet Engineering Task Force (IETF), tackles the more day-to-day issues of Internet operations. In spite of all this volunteerism and the lack of one central authority figure, the Internet runs just fine. The Internet caretakers, if you will, have proven quite ably that success does not have to depend on your typical top-down management team.

Likewise, the Internet's funding system may seem odd. There is a common misconception that the Internet is by its very nature free, but this is certainly not the case. It costs a pretty penny to maintain a machine that can serve up stuff on the Internet, and someone has to pay those costs. Individual groups and institutions—such as the federal government (via the National Science Foundation), which runs NSFNet—do indeed pay to provide the information they serve on the Internet. At the other end, new users quickly find out that connecting to the Internet through a service provider (such as Netcom, CRL, or PSI) requires a monthly usage fee; and because it is necessary to connect through a phone line, telephone charges may also be involved. Meanwhile, in the middle, the service providers pay for leasing high-speed communication lines; they also pay to access the Commercial Internet Exchange, and they may even pay to access a regional Internet provider such as BARRNet. As you can see, the Internet is by no means free, although it is a great value.

The funding issue is directly tied to how the Internet can be used. Because NSFNet (like ARPAnet) is funded by the federal government, its use is controlled for education and research and does not really permit commercial activities. (Exact guidelines for use of NSFNet are outlined in a document called the Acceptable Use Policy (AUP), which is available—like most items these days—on the Internet.) The good news is that these restrictions are gradually being relaxed, and that with the addition of new networks such as the Commercial Internet Exchange (CIX), created specifically for commercial traffic, the Internet is experiencing a boom in use for the sake of business. The Internet, then, is becoming commercialized. To be sure, it is this entre-preneurial business spirit which is the driving force behind the expanding Internet today.

The basic concepts on which the Internet was founded have accounted for its ability to grow and handle more and more computers and users, which now happens on a daily basis. What started as a military experiment during the heyday of Cold War politics has turned into a world-wide resource, allowing millions of people to connect seamlessly to a far-flung web of computers and information. (See Figure 1.4.) Who among the Internet's initial creators could have envisioned where we are today?

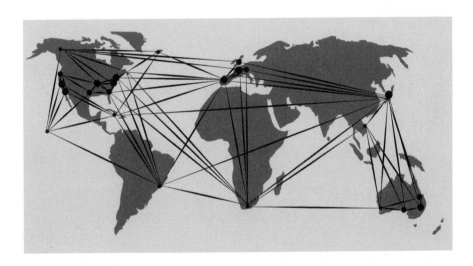

FIGURE 1.4: The Internet is a global resource, with servers on every continent.

What You Can Do with the Internet

Once you are connected to the Internet, here are some of the things you can do:

◆ Send messages to friends and associates all over the world with *e-mail*. (Remarkably, this usually does not involve long-distance charges to you or the recipient; all you're charged for is the call to your Internet service provider and, if that's a local number, it's a *local call*.)

◆ Exchange ideas with other people in a public forum with *Usenet*. (Note that unlike e-mail, which is more or less private, Usenet is public. Everyone else using Usenet can read what you post there. Also, while Usenet is not actually part of the Internet, it is accessible through most Internet providers.)

◆ Copy files from and to computers on the Internet with *FTP*. Many giant software archives, such as the CICA Windows archive, hold literally gigabytes of files you can retrieve.

◆ Connect to other computers on the Internet with *telnet*. (In order to connect to another computer, you need permission to use the computer.)

◆ Traverse and search directories of information with *gopher*.

◆ Search far and near for information on the Internet with the services *Archie*, *Veronica*, and *Jughead*.

◆ View documents, browse, search for data, and traverse other resources on the Internet via the *World Wide Web*.

Many of these tools are used (either visibly or behind the scenes) in the course of using Air Mosaic, so we'll talk about each one as it arises in later chapters.

The Internet as Medium

The Internet itself is just a medium. There's plenty of room to develop services to be used to make the most of the Internet, just as happened

What's Out There?

Air Mosaic provides limited support for e-mail in that Web documents can include links that allow you to send e-mail to the document's author (or anyone else the author chooses). More on this later.... The Internet itself, however, provides a number of resources you can use via Air Mosaic for finding people's e-mail addresses. You can look at the URL `gopher://gopher.tc.umn.edu/11/Phone%20Books/other` to search for people that have recently posted to Usenet. The URL `gopher://gopher.tc.umn.edu/11/Phone%20Books` includes links to many other databases of e-mail addresses.

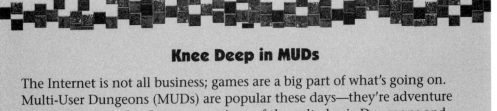

Knee Deep in MUDs

The Internet is not all business; games are a big part of what's going on. Multi-User Dungeons (MUDs) are popular these days—they're adventure games that started as Internet versions of the cult-classic Dungeons and Dragons. Some educational MUDs have also cropped up, but they all hold to the basic tenet of MUDs in that you interface with things in a world of fantasy. Unfortunately, you cannot access MUDs straight from Air Mosaic...at least not yet.

when the phone system was devised for simple communication and then many products and services were developed to take advantage of its potential (ranging from voicemail, pagers, and automated banking to the 911 system and, in fact, the Internet).

The Internet's fundamental openness has been responsible for bringing forth a number of tools for use by the masses. A great example of this is, of course, the original Mosaic. In the next chapter, we'll look at how you can access the best of the Internet—the World Wide Web—via Air Mosaic.

Best of the Internet: The World Wide Web via Air Mosaic

Before we leap head first into using Air Mosaic, an appreciation of the World Wide Web is in order. Let's take a quick look at the Web, then we'll glance at a typical Air Mosaic session and, still in this chapter, we'll talk more about what Air Mosaic can do.

How the Web Came to Be

The World Wide Web (a.k.a. WWW, W3, or simply, *the Web*) was originally developed to help physicists at Conseil Européen pour la Recherche Nucleaire (CERN), which is the European particle physics laboratory in Geneva, Switzerland. CERN is one of the world's largest scientific labs, composed of two organizations straddling the Swiss-French border: the European Laboratory for High Energy Physics in Switzerland, and the Organisation Européen pour la Recherche Nucleaire in France. The physicists there needed a way to exchange data and research materials quickly with other scientists.

The Web technology developed at CERN by Tim Berners-Lee enabled collaboration among members of research teams scattered all over the globe. How? Through a system that allows for *hypertext* links between documents on different computers.

Unlike regular documents, with static information on every page, *hypertext* documents have links built in so that readers can jump to more information about a topic by (typically) simply clicking on the word or picture identifying the item. That's why they call it hypertext—it's not just text, it's *hyper*text. (The term hypertext was coined by computer iconoclast Ted Nelson.) Hypertext is what makes Air Mosaic—and many multimedia tools—possible. The term *hypermedia* is sometimes used to refer to hypertext with the addition of other data formats. In addition to just text, Air Mosaic, equipped with the proper external programs, can support graphics, sound, and video.

Before going to CERN, Berners-Lee had worked on document production and text processing, and had developed for his own use a hypertext system—Enquire—in 1980. (According to some reports, he wasn't aware of the notion of hypertext at the time, but hypertext has been around since the Xanadu project in the 1960s.)

In 1992, the Web grew beyond the confines of the CERN's research community, and in just two years, its use and growth have been increasing exponentially. This was all part of the plan in a sense—the Web was meant to allow for open access—but it's hard to imagine that anyone could have expected the phenomenon that's occurred. Activity on the server at CERN doubles every four months, which is twice the rate of Internet expansion. At last count, it was estimated that there were over 2,000 Web servers worldwide, although official counts are impossible to do, given the size of the Web and the magnitude of its expansion.

Protocols, HTTP, and Hypertext: What It All Means

The Web's rapid expansion can be attributed in part to its extensive use of hypertext, held together by the HyperText Transfer Protocol (HTTP). A *protocol* is an agreed upon system for passing information back and forth that allows the transaction to be efficient (HTTP is a *network protocol*, which means it's a protocol for use with networks).

On Versions and Distributions

The original Mosaic, which was developed by Marc Andreessen and a team of programmers at the National Center for Supercomputing Applications (NCSA), was X Mosaic for Unix workstations. Since then, versions of NCSA Mosaic have become available for Windows-based PCs and the Macintosh. NCSA Mosaic was, for a time, distributed freely via the Net itself—anyone could download and use the software without charge. Those were the days. On the other hand, it wasn't easy for Internet novices to get and use the sofware—it was a pain even for experienced users to set up all the software needed to use NCSA Mosaic. That's where Spry's Air Mosaic comes in.

In mid-1994 NCSA began to license the rights to version 1.x of the software to other (often commercial) organizations. (NCSA is still developing version 2.) These organizations are allowed, by virtue of their licensing agreements with NCSA, to enhance the software. They can then distribute the enhanced software (called a *distribution*), and they can license others to distribute the sofware along with whatever enhancements they've included in their distribution. All distributions based on the original NCSA Mosaic have the word *Mosaic* in their names.

Included with this book, you'll find on disk a product called Spry Mosaic. The functional equivalent of Mosaic in a Box, and of CompuServe's WebLauncher, it's a fully integrated solution that you can just plug in and start to use. Spry Mosaic includes Air Mosaic, Spry's acclaimed, enhanced distribution of NCSA Mosaic. Spry Mosaic also includes instant Internet service (through CompuServe's specialized network) with over 400 local access phone numbers from which to choose.

Throughout this book we're concentrating on the distribution of Mosaic known as Air Mosaic, which is contained in the software package called Spry Mosaic.

Here's how this goes: if you (the *client*) go into a fast food place, the counterperson (the *server*) says, "May I help you?" You answer something like, "I'll have a Big Burger with cheese, fries, and a cola." Then he or she verifies your order by repeating it, tells you the cost, and concludes the transaction by trading food for cash. Basically, when you walk into any fast food place, you'll follow that same pattern and so will the person who takes your order. That's because you both know the *protocol*. The fast food protocol is part of what makes it "fast food."

In just that way, HTTP, which is the protocol that was developed as part of the Web project, enables the kinds of network conversations that need to occur quickly between computers so that leaps can be made from one document to another. You can use other protocols to do the same things HTTP does (Mosaic is *open-ended*, meaning that it's designed to support other network protocols as well as HTTP), but HTTP is terrifically efficient at what it does.

Information from around the Globe

The Web, as we've mentioned, is a network of global proportions. To ensure the continued success of the Web, the W3 Organization, headed jointly by CERN and by MIT's Laboratory for Computer Science (LCS), acts as the formal policy body and guiding light for the Web. The relationship between CERN and MIT/LCS as policy directors of the Web was formalized in June 1994 when both organizations announced an "international initiative for a universal framework for the information Web." The goal of the W3 Organization is to further the development and standardization of the World Wide Web, to make the global network easier to use for research, commerce, and future applications.

Web servers are located in many countries around the world, providing information on any topic you might imagine; a typical session using the Web might lead you through several continents. For example, research in the field of psychology may start at Yale and end up at a research hospital in Brussels, all within a few mouse-clicks that lead you along a series of hypertext links from a file at one location to another somewhere else.

The caveat here is that links are forged by the people who publish the information, and they may not make the same kinds of connections you would. That's why it's important to keep an open mind as you adventure around in the Web— just as you would when browsing in a library. You never know what you'll stumble across while you're looking for something else; conversely, you might have to do a bit of looking around to find exactly what you're seeking.

Who Makes This Information Available

Much of the information published on the Web exists thanks to the interest (and kindness) of the academic and research community; almost all the available information about the Web (and the Internet) is available through the work of that community. Files are stored on computers in research centers, hospitals, universities, and so on.

Increasingly, the Web is a forum for commercial use. Given that the telephone system did not fully develop for personal use until it was seen by commerce as a tool for business, we see commercial use of the Web as a positive development. So far, most commercial users of the Web have adhered to the Internet philosophy in that they give to the Internet as well as using it.

Anyone can become a Web publisher, as you'll see in Chapter 7. The Web software was developed at CERN on a NeXT computer, but has since been ported to many different platforms, including Macs, machines running Microsoft Windows, and others running versions of Unix and Linux. Rules about how to participate in publishing information on the Web are available from a variety of sources on the Internet, including the Web itself.

What's Out There?

Software you can use to set up a Web server on a Windows workstation is available via the URL `ftp://ftp.ncsa.uiuc.edu/Web/ httpd/Windows`. This will get you into a subdirectory from NCSA at the University of Illinois at Urbana-Champaign (UIUC); the software can be downloaded via anonymous FTP.

Web servers can be set up for strictly in-house purposes, too. For example, a large organization with massive amounts of internal documentation might publish its data for technical support staff using the HTTP service. This makes it possible to expand the idea of *in-house* to mean not just "in the building" but "company-wide." Just as members of a research team can use the Web to collaborate without having to be in the same location, so can members of a company's workgroup.

What's Out There?

You can retrieve information about creating and publicizing your Web documents from `http://www.pcweek.ziff.com/~eamonn/ crash_course.html`.

What Types of Information Exist

CERN also maintains the *Virtual Library*, a hypertext document that lists all resources by subject (see Figure 2.1). This may be a good point of entry for your first plunge into the Web if you just want to see what's out there. The hypertext page you'll see when you access the Virtual Library presents an alphabetized list of starting points for research. Topics cover standard academic research areas like Anthropology, Computer Science, and Literature; they branch out to Movies and Music; and they even include such esoterica as Fortune Telling.

What's Out There?

You can access the Virtual Library using the URL
`http://info.cern.ch/hypertext/DataSources/`
`bySubject/Overview.html`.

The WWW Virtual Library

This is a distributed subject catalogue. See **Summary**, **Library of Congress Classification** (Experimental), Top Ten most popular Fields (Experimental), Statistics (Experimental), and Index. See also arrangement by service type, and other subject catalogues of network information.

Mail to maintainers of the specified subject or www-request@info.cern.ch to add pointers to this list, or if you would like to contribute to administration of a subject area.

See also how to put your data on the web. All items starting with ! are *NEW!* (or newly maintained).

Aboriginal Studies
   This document keeps track of leading information facilities in the field of Australian Aboriginal studies as well as the Indigenous Peoples studies.
Aeronautics and Aeronautical Engineering
Agriculture
 ! Animal health, wellbeing, and rights
Anthropology
Applied Linguistics
Archaeology
Architecture
Art
Asian Studies
 ! Astronomy and Astrophysics
Aviation

FIGURE 2.1: Here you see a page from CERN's Virtual Library, a good index from which to start your exploration of the Web.

The Web has quickly moved beyond the world of academia and research, with more and more commercial applications appearing all the time. Large hardware and software vendors often publish price lists, monthly sales figures, and technical support information—for example, Dell Computer's Web service includes a "Solve Your Own Problem" section.

What's Out There?

A growing number of high-tech companies are making information available on the Web. Some familiar names—Microsoft, Novell, and Sybex—all maintain a presence on the Web. You can access these companies' home pages by using the URLs:

```
http://www.microsoft.com
http://www.novell.com
ftp://ftp.netcom.com/pub/sy/sybex/sybex.html
```

Other nonacademic, consumer-oriented Web servers (see Figure 2.2) include San Francisco Bay Area Parent Magazine, which provides on the Web lots of information of interest to all parents. MCA Records set up a "Woodstock '94" informational Web site, (but alas, with no hyperlinks to the original event.) You can take a tour of Graceland via the Web, finding photos of the "King" and listening to sound clips of Elvis music, and you can even order a pizza using a Web order form. (This last is a pilot project so far; the pizza will be delivered only if you live in Santa Cruz, California. Solamente in California, eh?) We'll show you how to explore these and many other places in Chapter 5.

What's Out There?

We accessed Woodstock '94 and Parent Magazine with the URLs
`http://metaverse.com/woodstock/index.html` and
`http://www.internet-is.com/parent/`.

The Role of the Browser

So far we've talked mainly about the structure and content of the Web, describing some of the information and links that make up the Web. So how does one jump into this Web and start cruising? You need a tool called a *browser*.

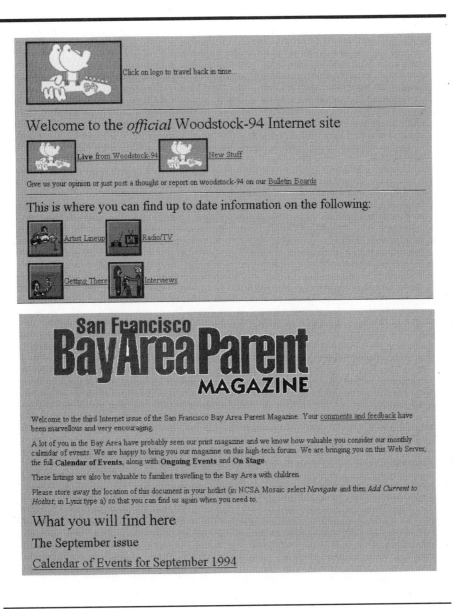

FIGURE 2.2:   Many companies see the Web as a way to put their messages in front of a wide audience. The home page above was set up by MCA Records for Woodstock '94; the one below was set up by Parent Magazine to provide information to parents.

A Couple of Caveats Sitting around Talking

Remember that the Web is ever-changing by its very nature. In this book, we attempt to guide you toward a lot of home pages that seem stable. Some others are just so interesting or unusual we can't pass them up, though. If you don't find a site we've described, it may be that it has gone the way of all things. Not to worry; something even more remarkable will probably crop up elsewhere. Another thing is that in the growing, ever-expanding Web, many of the servers you encounter may not be complete—their links may be "under construction." You'll usually see a warning if that's the case, along with an admonition to wear a hard hat.

Now at the risk of sounding like the nerds we've said you don't have to be, a browser, in technical terms, is a client process running on your computer that accesses a server process—in the case of the Web, the HTTP service—over the network. This is what's being discussed when people describe the Web as being based on client-server technology.

More simply put, the browser establishes contact with the server, reads the files—hypertext documents—made available on the HTTP server, and displays that stuff on your computer.

The document displayed by the browser is a hypertext document that contains references (or *pointers*) to other documents, which are very likely on other HTTP servers. These pointers are also called *links*. When you select a link from a hypertext page, the browser sends the request to the new server, which displays on your machine yet another document full of links.

In the same way you and a waiter at a restaurant have a client-server relationship when you ask for and receive water, a browser and the Web have a client-server relationship. The browser sends requests over the network to the Web server, which then provides a screenful of information back to your computer.

Before Mosaic was developed, all of this had to be accomplished using text-based browsers—the basic difference between them and Mosaic is just like the difference between PC programs written for DOS and those written for Windows. (DOS is text-based, so using DOS requires you to type in commands to see and use text-filled screens; Windows, like Mosaic, is graphical, so all you have to do is point and click on menu items and icons to see and use more graphically presented screens.) Figure 1.1 in Chapter 1 shows two views of the same information—one viewed with a text-based browser, the other with Mosaic.

How Mosaic Fits In

Often called the Internet's "Swiss Army knife," Mosaic is today's most popular World Wide Web browser. It was developed originally by the Software Development Group (SDG) at the National Center for Supercomputing Applications (NCSA), which is at the University of Illinois at Urbana-Champaign. In early 1993, research for developing an easy-to-use way to access the Internet led programmers there to explore the World Wide Web and the use of the HyperText Markup Language (HTML). HTML was being used for marking up documents on the Web—it's HTML that is used to *make* the document; Mosaic simply allows you to look at it easily.

Remember: Spry's Air Mosaic, the software that comes with this book, is an enhanced form of the more generic Mosaic developed by NCSA. Spry's Air Mosaic adds wonderful ease-of-use features and truly plug-and-play access to the Internet via a specialized CompuServe Internet access account.

HTML, a mark-up language with which text can be made to look like a page, is the coding scheme used in hypertext documents that both handles the text formatting on screen and makes it possible to create *links* to other documents, graphics, sound, and movies. Figure 2.3 shows an Air Mosaic document and the HTML coding that was used to create the document.

Remember, though, that Air Mosaic is not just a way to look at nice documents on the Internet. It also provides search capabilities within a hypertext document through links. We'll get into this more and more as we go along....

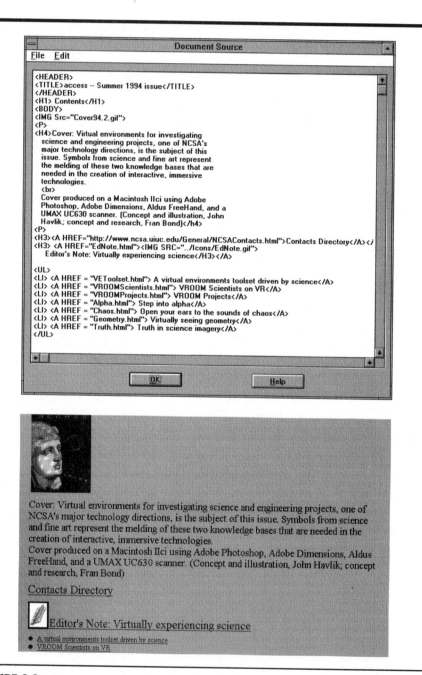

```
┌─────────────────────── Document Source ───────────────────────┐
│ File   Edit                                                     │
├─────────────────────────────────────────────────────────────┤
<HEADER>
<TITLE>access -- Summer 1994 issue</TITLE>
</HEADER>
<H1> Contents</H1>
<BODY>
<IMG Src="Cover94.2.gif">
<P>
<H4>Cover: Virtual environments for investigating
    science and engineering projects, one of NCSA's
    major technology directions, is the subject of this
    issue. Symbols from science and fine art represent
    the melding of these two knowledge bases that are
    needed in the creation of interactive, immersive
    technologies.
    <br>
    Cover produced on a Macintosh IIci using Adobe
    Photoshop, Adobe Dimensions, Aldus FreeHand, and a
    UMAX UC630 scanner. (Concept and illustration, John
    Havlik; concept and research, Fran Bond}</h4>
<P>
<H3><A HREF="http://www.ncsa.uiuc.edu/General/NCSAContacts.html">Contacts Directory</A></
<H3> <A HREF="EdNote.html"><IMG SRC="../Icons/EdNote.gif">
    Editor's Note: Virtually experiencing science</H3></A>

<UL>
<LI> <A HREF = "VEToolset.html"> A virtual environments toolset driven by science</A>
<LI> <A HREF = "VROOMScientists.html"> VROOM Scientists on VR</A>
<LI> <A HREF = "VROOMProjects.html"> VROOM Projects</A>
<LI> <A HREF = "Alpha.html"> Step into alpha</A>
<LI> <A HREF = "Chaos.html"> Open your ears to the sounds of chaos</A>
<LI> <A HREF = "Geometry.html"> Virtually seeing geometry</A>
<LI> <A HREF = "Truth.html"> Truth in science imagery</A>
</UL>

            ┌────────┐              ┌────────┐
            │   OK   │              │  Help  │
            └────────┘              └────────┘
```

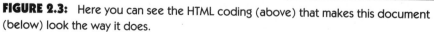

Cover: Virtual environments for investigating science and engineering projects, one of NCSA's major technology directions, is the subject of this issue. Symbols from science and fine art represent the melding of these two knowledge bases that are needed in the creation of interactive, immersive technologies.
Cover produced on a Macintosh IIci using Adobe Photoshop, Adobe Dimensions, Aldus FreeHand, and a UMAX UC630 scanner. (Concept and illustration, John Havlik; concept and research, Fran Bond)

Contacts Directory

Editor's Note: Virtually experiencing science

● A virtual environments toolset driven by science
● VROOM Scientists on VR

FIGURE 2.3: Here you can see the HTML coding (above) that makes this document (below) look the way it does.

Looking into HTML

If you want to see what HTML looks like, while you are viewing a document in Air Mosaic, you can select File ➤ Document Source from Air Mosaic's menu bar. A window will open showing the HTML for that document. You can't change the HTML you see, but you can copy pieces of it, or even the whole thing, to your Windows Clipboard (highlight what you want and press Ctrl-C) or you can save it as a text file to your local machine. (See Chapter 3.) Click on OK when you're done, and your view will once more be the document as it appears in Air Mosaic.

Using Air Mosaic to Access World Wide Web Information

Air Mosaic lets you browse the information available on the Web just as you might browse the shelves of the New York Public Library. In fact, Air Mosaic makes it so you can easily and quickly browse *entire rooms* of shelves, and the Web makes available literally thousands of "rooms" in "libraries" as expansive as the New York Public. Using Air Mosaic, you can skim material quickly or you can stop and delve into topics as deeply as you wish. Let's take a quick look at an Air Mosaic session in action.

A Typical Air Mosaic Session

In our sample session, let's look for information about the Rolling Stones.

 This is a <u>sample</u> session; it's here to give you an idea of how things go. We'll talk in more detail in later chapters about how to accomplish various things using Air Mosaic.

To start Air Mosaic, we double-click on the Air Mosaic icon in the Windows Program Manager. The Internet connection is established automatically, and the start-up home page (Figure 2.4) appears on screen. From here we can traverse the Web by clicking on links, which appear on the home page as pictures and as underlined words in blue.

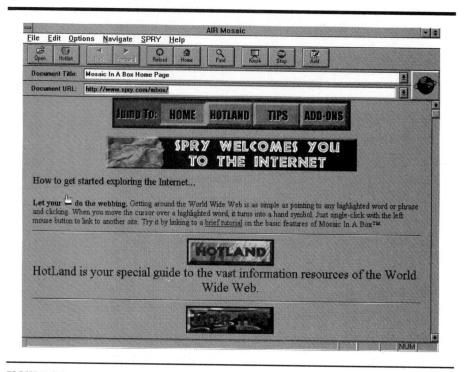

FIGURE 2.4:   The default start-up home page includes some very handy links.

Let's say in an earlier session we found the NCSA home page. There we clicked on What's New and we got the NCSA What's New document. Near the top of this document we found a link (appearing as a word in blue) that said something like "search back documents," which led us to the CUI W3 Catalog, which is actually stored on a machine at CERN, in Switzerland. The CUI W3 Catalog is a catalog of announcements of new services and information available on the Web. Its URL was shown at the top of the screen while we were viewing the catalog, we stored the URL in Air Mosaic's Hotlist (more on this in Chapter 3) so we could find it easily again when we wanted to.

What's Out There?

The CUI W3 Catalog is not the only catalog of resources on the Web, but it is one of the most useful, and is always a good place to start your search. Its URL is `http://cuiwww.unige.ch/w3catalog`.

To open the CUI W3 Catalog without retracing all of the steps we went through when we discovered the catalog, we select File ➤ Open URL. The Open URL dialog box appears.

From our previous session, we know the URL; now we can type this into the URL text box, then press ↵. After a few seconds, the document is transferred from Switzerland and displayed on screen. You can see it in Figure 2.5.

To go on with our research on the Rolling Stones, we type into the space next to the Submit button a term to search for, in our case "Rolling Stones." Then we click on the Submit button to activate the search. It may take a minute to search the database (it's a *big* database). Once the search is done, the results appear on screen (Figure 2.5).

CUI W3 Catalog

Please enter a search word/pattern or provide a Perl regular expression:

| Submit | |

NB: Searches are case-insensitive.

Result of search for "Rolling Stones":

September 2, 1994: The World's Greatest Rock 'n' Roll Band is proud to announce their very own Web Server. They are the Rolling Stones and they are now giving you the best place in netland for the real Stones fan to hang out. Offerings include:

- live audio
- live video
- exclusive photos
- official merchandise
- pure text

All from their 94/95 Voodoo Lounge World Tour. (nwn)

This file was generated by htgrep v1.5.

FIGURE 2.5: Searching the CUI W3 Catalog for the term "Rolling Stones" finds this entry about the Rolling Stones Web server.

The first entry we see starts, "The World's Greatest Rock 'n' Roll Band is proud to announce their very own Web server," and goes on to say that the Rolling Stones now have a Web server with information about their Voodoo Lounge tour. In that description the phrase "Rolling Stones" is in blue—it's a link to the server's home page. We click on the link to access the Rolling Stones Web server and the Rolling Stones home page appears. You can see it in Figure 2.6.

The Rolling Stones home page is our entry point to scads of information about the Voodoo Lounge tour (and perhaps by the time you read this, even more). Here we can click on links to view backstage snapshots, video clips of performances, a schedule of performance dates, and a catalog of stuff to buy.

With our curiosity about the Stones satisfied, we can exit the program directly from wherever we happen to be, by selecting File ➤ Exit from Air Mosaic's menu bar.

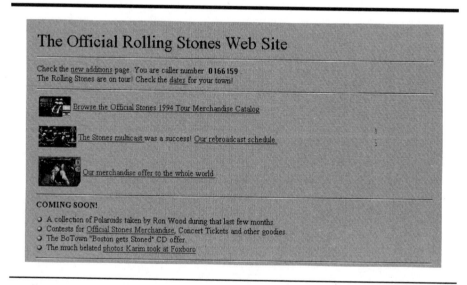

FIGURE 2.6: The Rolling Stones home page (after we scrolled down below the opening graphics)

How Data Travels

Spry Mosaic—the software that includes Air Mosaic and comes with this book—is about as easy to install and start as it can be (see the appendix). But you can't usually just install other forms of Mosaic on your Windows computer and expect them simply to work. It's worth taking a look at this for a few minutes. The interface mechanism between the client (Mosaic) and the Web server (the machine dishing up the information you want to view) depends on the Internet protocol known as TCP/IP (Transmission Control Protocol/Internet Protocol). TCP/IP creates *packets* (see Figure 2.7)—which are like electronic envelopes to carry data on a network—and then places the packets on the network. It also makes it possible, of course, to receive packets.

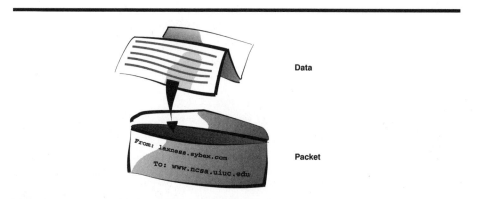

Data

Packet

FIGURE 2.7:   Data (e-mail, documents, video, whatever) travels across the Internet in packets.

The Domain Name System and Packets

There is a system responsible for administering and keeping track of domains and (believe it or not) it's called the Domain Name System (DNS for short). DNS is a distributed system that administers names by allowing different groups control over subsets of names. In this system, there can be many levels or domains, but the top-level domains are generally standardized, making it easy for mail to be routed.

E-Mail Addressing

Electronic mail, or e-mail, is the established form of communication on the Internet. In fact, typically this is where most of us encounter the Internet for the first time. A friend tells you his Internet e-mail address at work is `kmfez@schwartz.com`, and asks for your e-mail address, and you begin exchanging messages that magically pop up in your on-screen e-mail in-basket. Users around the country—for that matter, around the world—readily grasp e-mail as a quick, convenient means for conducting research or just for staying in touch (and for doing so without the expense associated with a long-distance phone call).

How does e-mail work? It's actually a lot like the Postal Service. E-mail uses addressing and a "store and forward" mechanism. This means that there is a standard way of addressing, and the mail is routed from one place to another until ultimately it appears at its destination. Along the way, if necessary, a machine can store the mail until it knows how to forward it.

Of course, there is a little more than that to sending e-mail on its way, but not much. The address in your e-mail header, much like the address on a postal letter, contains all the information necessary to deliver the message to the recipient. In the world of the Internet, a person's e-mail address is made up of two parts: a user name and a computer name, indicating where the user's ID is located.

In the example `kmfez@schwartz.com`, `kmfez` is the user portion of the address, and `schwartz.com` is the name of the location (actually a host machine). The last part of the location's name, `.com`, is known as the *high-level domain*—in this case `.com` tells you that it is a *com*mercial organization. If `.edu` appeared instead, you'd know it was an *edu*cational organization.

An address can actually contain many domains, which you see separated by periods, like this: `joke.on.you.com`. If more than one domain appears in an address, they move in hierarchy from left to right. As you read to the right, the domains get larger in scope.

In addition to the more familiar "English" names, all machines on the Internet have an Internet address in the form of four numbers separated by decimals; this is because, while a user might change the "English" address, an address is needed that will never change. This numeric address is organized in a system commonly called *dotted decimal notation*. An example of a host computer's address would be 130.19.252.21. These numeric addresses work fine for machines communicating with each other, but most people find them cumbersome to use and tricky to remember. To help people out, host computers were given names, such as *ruby* or *topaz*, making it easier to remember and to facilitate connecting.

However, other factors came into play, such as making sure that each machine on the Internet had a unique name, registering the names in a centrally managed file, and distributing the file to everyone on the Internet. This system worked adequately when the Internet was still small, but as it grew in size, so did the size of the file keeping track of all the host names.

The common standard American domains are as follows:

com	Commercial business, company, or organization
edu	Educational institution (university, etc.)
gov	Nonmilitary government site
mil	Military site
net	Any host associated with network administration, such as a gateway
org	Private organization (nonacademic, nongovernmental, and noncommercial)

These domains are referred to as *descriptive* domains. In addition, each country also has its own top-level domain, commonly called a *geographical*

domain. Here in the United States, we are in the us domain. Other examples of countries represented with domains include:

au	Australia
ca	Canada
fr	France

Just as you need not know the internal workings of the U.S. Postal Service and its every machine to use the system and get your mail, you don't need to know all about TCP/IP to use Mosaic. But it does help to have some understanding.

TCP/IP is not part of Mosaic; it's part of your local network if you're on one. If you're not on a local network, though—if, for example, you're using your stand-alone machine at home or at work—you can still use Mosaic. In that case, you have to have special network drivers loaded (not to worry, Spry Mosaic includes them) to make things go back and forth over the phone connection using the protocol Mosaic understands.

One of the many great things about Spry Mosaic, the software that includes Air Mosaic and that comes with this book, is that it takes care of this TCP/IP business so you don't have to worry about making the connection work.

What Air Mosaic Recognizes

Air Mosaic has many big selling points, one of which is that it provides one-stop shopping for the Web by handling a variety of data types. Data types are just that—types of data. Having standard types of data makes it possible for one machine (indeed, a program) to recognize and use data that was created on another machine (and maybe even in another program).

The data types recognized by Air Mosaic include:

- ◆ HTML
- ◆ Graphics
- ◆ Sound
- ◆ Video

The data type that the Web was designed around is HTML, the type the HyperText Transfer Protocol we've talked so much about was designed to transfer.

HTTP servers, the servers that make up the World Wide Web, serve hypertext documents (coded with HTML, as we've discussed). These documents are not just what you view; it's actually these HTML documents that guide you through the Web when you're cruising.

When you view hypertext documents using a line-mode browser (see Figure 1.1), you'll see the links displayed as item numbers, or as reverse-video, depending upon your display. When you view hypertext documents using Air Mosaic, you'll see the links displayed as text that's either underlined or in a different color than the main text in the document.

Clicking on the underlined or colored text pops you to the next link, which may be another hypertext document or a graphic, or even a sound or video file.

Air Mosaic's Use of Viewers

For those data types that it can't handle directly, Air Mosaic uses external "viewers." (In this context, a *viewer* is software that might specialize in displaying a graphic or playing a sound, a movie, or both.) Viewers are independent applications developed for viewing, opening, or accessing a particular type of information.

Again, as part of setting up any other Mosaic, you'd have to configure it to work with specific viewers. Spry's Air Mosaic comes all set up with basic viewers; there are a few, however, you might want to add to your Air Mosaic toolkit. For example, you might configure audio files to be played by WHAM, a Windows-based audio application that's available as freeware.(See Chapter 8.)

How Viewers Work

Briefly, here's how viewers work: Air Mosaic looks at the first line (the *header*) in the file; the header tells Air Mosaic what it needs to know to deal with the file appropriately. Text files are displayed on screen, in the very attractive way Air Mosaic displays them. Compressed files, such as graphics, are uncompressed and then displayed. But when Air Mosaic encounters a sound or video file, the program "knows" it needs help and it launches the appropriate viewer to "play" the file—if you have the viewer on your machine, you won't see much evidence of this; you'll just hear the sound or see the movie on screen.

Many viewers are available in the public domain from many Internet sources (including anonymous FTP servers and the Web) and for all types of files. NCSA makes it clear that it neither maintains nor formally distributes the viewers needed to work with the various files that the different Mosaics can access, but when NCSA learns of a viewer that can be freely distributed, they file a copy of it on a server in Illinois. (We'll tell you how to get and use viewers in Chapter 8.)

 With the help of viewers, you can play sound and video clips with Air Mosaic, but be prepared to wait a while for the files to be transferred. Most sound and video files are multi-megabytes in size. As a rough estimate, each megabyte takes about 15 minutes to transfer with a 14.4K bps modem (that is, on a good day with prevailing winds). It might take literally hours to access a single, relatively short video clip.

Let's talk for a minute about those types of data Air Mosaic most commonly needs a viewer to work with. (We'll go into more detail about how to use this stuff in Chapter 8.)

Graphics Usually when you encounter graphics while using Air Mosaic, they'll be one of two kinds: those that appear in the document, which Air Mosaic needs no help to work with, and those that require you click on something in order to view them. To work with these, Air Mosaic needs the help of an external viewer.

Wanderers, Spiders, and Robots—Oh My!

In June 1993, there were about 130 Web servers on the Internet. Six months later, there were over 200. Two months after that, there were over 600. By April 1994, there were over 1,200; in December 1994 the number hit 2,000. So, how do you find what you need in this ever-expanding haystack? Wouldn't it be great to know what's out on the Web, and where?

You can find out, by consulting World Wide Web creatures known as *wanderers*, *spiders*, or *robots*. An assortment of Web robots have been developed since the beginnings of the WWW; these programs travel through the Web and find HTTP files—the files that make up the content of the Web. With names the likes of Arachnophobia, W4, Webfoot Robot, JumpStation Robot, Repository-Based Software Engineering Project Spider, WebCrawler, WebLinker, and World Wide Web Worm, you may not see their useful purposes when you first encounter them.

Some robots, such as W4, were designed strictly to keep track of growth on the Web. The statistics cited at the beginning of this piece were gathered by W4; the W4 page of the Web keeps these figures posted and updated.

The more interesting and useful Web crawlers are those that dump the information they gather into a place that's readable by the rest of us browsers. The World Wide Web Worm is one such robot. The information is collected into an indexed database that Web users can search.

The Repository Based Software Engineering Project Spider creates an Oracle database by searching through links within the Web to find HTML files. The data that's extracted is then siphoned off into a WAIS index, which can be searched.

Check out Chapter 6 for information about accessing the World Wide Web Worm and some of these other robots.

Air Mosaic can work with many common types of graphic images, for example, GIF, TIFF, and JPEG. You don't really need to concern yourself with what the names of these formats mean, though, unless you plan to publish your own documents. Most of the time, all you'll be doing is looking at things; sometimes the graphic you'll see in your Air Mosaic document window is a link to another document or a larger, compressed image. Clicking on the picture will begin the process of bringing the other file over the network. For those you need a viewer.

Sound Air Mosaic must be configured in order to be able to play sound files; once it is configured, Windows audio files (WAV), Basic audio (AU), or MIDI (MID) files may be included as linked data. Remember that sound files can be very large and take a long time to transfer over a slow connection.

Video Air Mosaic can be configured to work with viewers for QuickTime movies (MOV), Microsoft video (AVI), and movie files compressed using the MPEG compression standard. Again, remember that many video files you'll come across as you begin to work with Air Mosaic are, in the words of Tiny Elvis, "huge."

Air Mosaic as a Consistent Interface to Other Internet Resources

In addition to providing a nice graphical user interface to linked multimedia information, Air Mosaic also provides a consistent interface to other information types available on the Internet. In fact, many of the links in the hypertext documents on the Web will take you to information on FTP servers, gopher servers, or WAIS servers. (Read on for the gory details.) You can also read newsgroups and post messages to them from Air Mosaic.

Let's take a quick look at the kinds of resources that make up the Web and that you can access using Air Mosaic.

FTP: For Transferring Files

We've talked about viewing files; actually obtaining them is a different matter. To transfer a file from one machine (a server, for example) to another (yours, for example) you need FTP. File Transfer Protocol (FTP) is one of the means by which you move files around the Internet. Both a communications protocol and an application, it is the application that is of most interest to many people, as we use FTP to obtain files (once we've located them, of course) from all kinds of Internet sources. This kind of file transfer most often works in what is known as *anonymous FTP* mode.

FTP itself only lets you see a list of the files on a computer, whereas Air Mosaic lets you see more—the files, but also the contents of the files, even graphics, sounds, movies, etc. Still, FTP should not be overlooked for what it has accomplished and still does, namely, allowing users to bring home files, information, and data that otherwise would be left for browsing only.

After retrieving the file, you may need to perform some additional steps if the file has been compressed to save space. This involves using a utility to uncompress, or unzip, the file to make it usable. There are many compression formats in use, so you may find yourself cursing sometimes rather than jumping for joy when you uncover just the file you are looking for but are unable to unzip it.

What's Out There?

You can retrieve a table listing available compression software with the URL `ftp://ftp.cso.uiuc.edu/doc/pcnet/compression`.

Air Mosaic presents FTP directories as a graphical menu using icons that are similar to those used by the Windows File Manager. Directories are represented by a folder icon; text files are displayed as the familiar sheet-of-paper-with-top-corner-folded-down. These items all appear as links—they are underlined so that you can click on them to move to the place in question.

Another advantage of Air Mosaic, over say a regular FTP session, is that Air Mosaic reads the file type, so it can display a text file on screen when you click on the link. A regular FTP session involves copying the file to your workstation and then opening it later using a text editor.

Likewise, Air Mosaic will deal with sound, image, and video files that appear as links (in the FTP list) as it does in other contexts, displaying the text, picture, or movie, or playing the sound when you click on the link.

Anonymous FTP Explained Here

Anonymous FTP permits users to access remote systems without actually having user accounts on the systems. In effect, it allows for "guests" to visit a remote site, and permits just enough computer privileges to access the resources provided. The process involves the user starting an FTP connection and logging in to the remote computer as the user "anonymous," with an arbitrary password which, for the purposes of Internet etiquette, should be your e-mail address. The beauty of using Air Mosaic for anonymous FTP is that you don't have to go through all the login steps, you don't have to use a text-based FTP program on your machine, and Air Mosaic displays all the stuff on the FTP server in an easy-to-use graphical interface. You can tell when a Web document you are viewing in Air Mosaic comes from an anonymous FTP site, because the URL starts with `ftp:`.

Air Mosaic must be properly configured with the appropriate external viewer applications in order to play sounds or movies and display pictures. Also, once Air Mosaic plays the sound or movie, it's gone. You'll learn how to save the images, sounds, and videos in Chapter 3.

Gopher: For Searching and Finding

When you use a URL in Air Mosaic that begins with gopher, your copy of Air Mosaic is talking to a gopher server. Originally developed at the University of Minnesota as a front-end to telnet and FTP, gopher has since caught on as one of the more important information retrieval tools on the Internet.

When you access gopher information with Air Mosaic you are presented with a series of menu choices, much like the directory structure one sees in the Microsoft Windows File Manager. By double-clicking on icons, you can traverse the directory structure a level at a time until you come to an item. The great thing about gopher is that you don't have to know what the item is, or even where it is (unlike FTP). If the item is a file to download, gopher invokes an FTP session. If the item is a link to another computer, gopher invokes a telnet session so you can use that computer. If it is something to be displayed—a graphic, a text document, etc.—it will do so on your screen, provided you have the proper client software installed on your PC. All this happens without the necessity of you worrying about Internet addressing schemes, domains, host names, and such.

The other aspect that makes gopher so powerful is that gopher servers reference or *point* to each other. It really doesn't matter where the data is located, or where you start accessing gopher servers, because gopher is able to take you there seamlessly. This is an obvious step up from using FTP, because with FTP you have to know the name of the FTP machine to get anything from it.

The University of Minnesota gopher server acts as the master gopher; by registering with the university, administrators can make their gopher server available through the master, thus allowing world-wide access to their servers. Note that there is not a gopher-formatted resource per se, rather, gopher acts as a helper to collect the Internet resources into a convenient inventory that lets you find items in much the same way you use the subject card catalogs at a library. In fact, with the way the gopher servers reference one another, all this information almost appears to be on one gigantic computer.

When you use Air Mosaic, gopher server information is presented as a graphical menu listing of folders and file icons—just like FTP server files. (See Figure 2.8.) Because gopher data is indexed, however, you can perform a

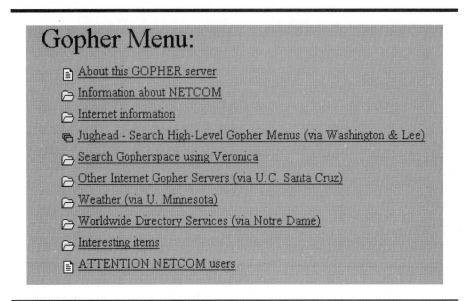

FIGURE 2.8: When you use Air Mosaic to access a gopher server, you will see folder and file icons much like those that appear in Windows File Manager.

gopher search. Air Mosaic has a Find menu option; when you select it, a dialog box will pop up to enable you to enter your search string. (This same dialog box appears regardless of what type of indexed data you're searching—it could just as well be hypertext or a WAIS database.)

WAIS: For Searching Text Databases

The Internet Wide Area Information Service, WAIS, lets you search indexed information to find articles containing groups of words you choose. WAIS is a lot like gopher, in that it shields you from having to know on what computer the information resides. Unlike gopher, WAIS does the searching for you. A WAIS search is not totally accomplished without some human intervention—someone has to make the text information available on a WAIS server by indexing it; but once that happens, anyone can gain access to it. From a WAIS client, you decide which library of information to search and which words to search on. WAIS then returns articles and documents containing those keywords.

There are a few drawbacks to WAIS. Since there are no special words, every word counts. That is, if you search the word *car*, everything containing any occurrence of that word is retrieved. And you can't narrow your search—there currently is no logical "and" operation, allowing you to look for, say, *Porsches and Ferraris*. Another problem is that you can't tell WAIS to discard articles that may have gone astray; you basically get a lot more at times than you bargained for, which means some sifting on your part is required. In spite of these small annoyances, WAIS is still one of the most useful search tools on the Internet today.

Air Mosaic lets you access WAIS servers through a WWW-WAIS gateway, which converts the data to the appropriate format for the Web. Of course, the beauty of Air Mosaic is, as usual, that you don't need to know about gateways or even WAIS itself to perform a search on WAIS indexes. Hypertext links may point to WAIS information. (See Figure 2.9.)

FIGURE 2.9: Using the CIA World-Factbook93 WAIS database, you can quickly find information about any country in the world.

Like other indexes (such as gopher), WAIS indexes display as searchable indexes.

Usenet: All the News You'd Ever Want

The first stop for new Internet browsers after e-mail typically used to be network news, although with the advent of graphical tools such as Mosaic, this may no longer be the case. (Air Mosaic provides limited access to newsgroups.)

Network news is the great question and answer, ask-and-you-shall-receive-a-reply oracle of this century. It is like e-mail in that you are reading and possibly replying to messages, but unlike it in that you are able to partake of a broader scope of public conversations and discussions, with as little or as much participation as you want. You don't even have to take part—you can just stand back and watch if you'd rather. There are literally thousands of discussion groups on nearly every subject imaginable; you can join in or just cruise through them as you like.

Network news occurs in a format a lot like that of a private BBS system, such as CompuServe. Because it is organized into newsgroups, it is very easy to work your way through the major headings and then through the newsgroups themselves. You need a newsreader, a piece of software that organizes and sorts the newsgroups—there are a number available for all the major platforms. You can even download them free from the Internet.

The major (but not the only) source of network news is Usenet, which is a free service. Usenet was actually born before the Internet, and much confusion exists as to how the two interact. Usenet is not a network like the Internet, there are no Usenet computers per se, and Usenet doesn't even need the Internet. Rather, what drives Usenet is akin to an agreement set up between those who want to distribute and those who want to read newsgroups. Network administrators arrange with other administrators to transfer newsgroups back and forth, which usually occurs via the Internet, but only because that's convenient. The site that provides your site with news is called a *news feed*. Some newsgroups end up being transferred by some computers, others by other computers, and so on.

Network news is accessible via many Mosaics through gateways from newsgroups to the Web. Some Mosaics work okay as newsreaders, but most don't let you respond to postings or post your own. Most Mosaics also won't let you subscribe or unsubscribe to newsgroups, nor keep track of the articles you've read versus those still unread.

 Spry's Air Mosaic not only works fine as a newsreader, but also lets you respond to postings and post your own. It is similar to other Mosaics, however, in that it doesn't let you subscribe or unsubscribe to your favorite newsgroup. You'll find more on Air Mosaic's newsgroup features in Chapter 3.

On the plus side for Mosaic, however, cross-references from one article to other articles are converted to links that make it easy to follow a conversational thread, which isn't always the case with newsreaders. Figure 2.10 shows links in a Web document.

Internet Newsgroups

This is a list of internet newsgroups. See also:
- About these lists, and reading news with W3 .
- Index of people who have contributed news .

alt
    Alternative Groups. The creation of these groups is not moderated.
bionet
    Biology.
bit
    Bitnet Gatewayed Goups
biz
    Comercially oriented (business)
cern
    CERN local interest groups. See also: fnal , hepnet .
ch
    Swiss newsgroups.
comp
    Computing. Many groups, on all aspects.
de
    German groups.
DESY
    DESY newsgroups.
eunet
    European Usenet newsgroups

Click here to jump to a list of Usenet newsgroups of this type.

FIGURE 2.10:   You will often find links to Usenet newsgroups in Web documents.

The Human Side of Hypermedia

The Web is hypermedia-based, which is why it is called the Web: the notion of interconnections and multiple branching points, no beginning and no end, is implicit in the Web. The structure of the information is not hierarchical or linear. The Web and its hypertext underpinnings offer a rich environment for exploring tangential or directly related information because the hypertext paradigm works the way people do when they're on the road to discovery.

For example, if you were a kid in the '60s or '70s working on a book report about Native American cultures, your process might have looked like this: you began by reading the encyclopedia section on *Indians* (this, remember, is before Native Americans were referred to as such) when you came to a passage describing the dislocation of the Hopi people to a reservation near what is today called Apache Junction, Arizona.

Having never been near Arizona, you decided to find out about its climate, terrain, flora and fauna. Putting the *I* volume aside on the floor, you grabbed the *A* volume and dipped into *Arizona*. Then you wondered, "What's it like today?" You called the Apache Junction Chamber of Commerce and asked for recent industrial and employment statistics. Later that day, curious about the status of any national reparations made to the Hopi in Arizona, you made a trip to your local library and had a chat with the reference librarian, who in turn brought you copies of various federal government policy statements.

Thus, the kind of discovery process supported by hypertext—and the Web—is really modeled after the way people tend to work when they're learning new things. Following our example using other tools on the Internet, such as gopher, would be like doing the research for your childhood book report by starting each search for a distinct bit of information from the table of contents of a single book. It's easy to see why the hypertext paradigm and the Web have really taken off. In a hypertext document, if you want more information about something you can just click on its link and there you are: the linked item could be a document on a server 7,500 miles away. If you were writing that book report today, you might travel all over the world, via the Web, without ever leaving your computer.

Moving Along...

With all this backstory in place, you're ready now to hit the highway. Starting with the next chapter, we're going to dig into how you do what you do with Air Mosaic and the Web. Let's hit the road.

Part Two:

Using Air Mosaic

Running Air Mosaic

Let's get working with Air Mosaic. In this chapter, you'll learn to start the product that came with this book, and then how to open and save documents, switch between documents and other hypermedia (sound and video, for example) via *hot links*, and finally how to save files to your local hard drive.

This chapter assumes you've already installed the Spry Mosaic package (included with this book) on your PC. When you install the software, you'll conveniently and automatically subscribe to CompuServe's specialized network, providing access to the Internet (this is not access to CompuServe information services, mind you). For fully detailed information on the easy process of installing the software, turn to the appendix at the back of this book.

● Launching Air Mosaic

Launching Air Mosaic is as easy as it can be. If you follow the installation directions in the appendix, an Air Mosaic icon will appear in its own special group in the Windows Program Manager. You don't have to first start up the software that will allow for network access and data transfer; to start Air Mosaic, in just one step:

1. Double-click on the Air Mosaic icon.

That's all there is to it.

SLIP and PPP: The Mosaic Connneciton

Launching Air Mosaic, the product included with this book, is a simple matter of double-clicking on an icon. Using Air Mosaic, you'll never know what a chore it once was to start the other Mosaics. If you were to run most forms of Mosaic on a stand-alone PC, you'd first have to start whatever software (SLIP or PPP) you were using to access the Internet, *then* start Mosaic. This is not the Internet service provider we're discussing—you'd need a service provider, but you'd *also* need SLIP or PPP software to form a vital connecting link between Mosaic and your Internet service provider. *Spry Mosaic, the software on the disk that includes Air Mosaic and comes with this book, includes that vital connecting software and Internet access.*

Here's how SLIP or PPP software works: you start your connection software—SLIP or PPP, whichever you have on your machine. (If you're using Spry's Air Mosaic, this is automatic.) Your connection software then contacts your Internet service provider (which is on a machine somewhere else) and they do a little dance together, passing back and forth the TCP/IP packets that make it possible for you to run Mosaic (which is on your machine). Voilà—a connection is created and the Internet accepts your machine as a little network hooked into the bigger, more exciting network called the Internet!

With Spry's Air Mosaic, it will appear that you have a direct connection to the Internet—PPP software is built into Spry Mosaic. That means you don't have to tend to all this connection software, you just click on words and pictures as you would using Windows, and everything happens. This makes cruising the Internet a really smooth experience.

You can also start Air Mosaic in the Windows File Manager by double-clicking on the filename AIRMOS.EXE, and if you want to make things really hard on yourself, you can (again in the Windows Program Manager) choose File ➤ Run and then type in the complete path and filename for Air Mosaic, for example, **c:\spry\bin\airmos.exe**.

If all goes well (and it surely will) the Air Mosaic window will open and the world icon in the window's upper-right corner will become animated.

This tells you that Air Mosaic is transferring data, which will appear in a second in the form of a home page. Whenever Mosaic is "working" (downloading a document, doing a search, and so on) the world is animated. It stops when the action has been completed.

The first time you start Air Mosaic, the first window you'll see is the default start-up home page (Figure 3.1). You can change the start-up home page to something else and we'll tell you how to do that later, in Chapter 4.

The home page is where you begin, where Air Mosaic first lands you on your Internet voyage. Think of it as one of many ports of entry into the Web—the Web, you'll recall, doesn't just go from here to there…it's literally a *web*. It doesn't really matter where you start, because everything's interconnected.

You can return to the start-up home page (the one you see when you start an Air Mosaic session) at any time simply by clicking on the home icon on the Air Mosaic tool bar.

If you followed the steps earlier in this chapter and have Air Mosaic running now, try clicking on the home icon. This brief exercise will test your

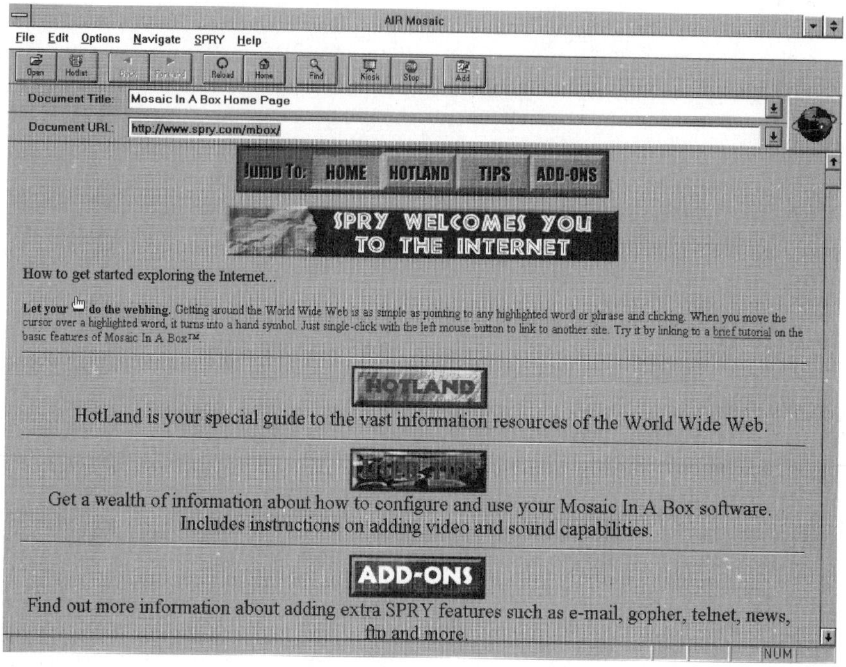

FIGURE 3.1: Spry Mosaic is the funcitonal equivalent of Mosaic in a Box. Here you can see the start-up home page to prove it.

Internet connection. The world should be animated and you should see the start-up home page displayed again on your screen.

What's Out There?

By default, the start-up home page is the Mosaic in a Box home page. This is because Spry Mosaic is the functional equivalent of Spry's Mosaic in a Box. If you change the start-up home page and want to find it again, its URL is http://www.spry.com/mbox.

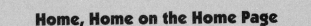

Home, Home on the Home Page

The start-up home page—any home page, for that matter— may be located anywhere on the Web. Home pages provide a lot of information and change frequently, so you may not want to zip by the start-up home page—take the time to review it when it pops up.

You can even make it so that Air Mosaic won't load a home page on startup. (See Chapter 4.) Either option is fine. You can also store any number of home pages that you find on the Internet. You are not limited to the start-up home page by any means—you can even create your own home page. Refer to Chapter 7 for instructions on how to do so.

What You See:
The Air Mosaic Interface

Let's look at the parts of the Air Mosaic window. The interface shows a window called the document view window. Figure 3.2 shows you what's what.

The tool bar, status bar, and the current URL bar can be displayed or hidden on your screen. They are activated or deactivated through the Configuration dialog box—from the menu bar, select Options ➤ Configuration and set things up as you like.

Title Bar In the title bar you can see the name of the client software itself.

Menu Bar The menu bar is similar to those in other Windows applications: it provides you with pull-down menus. When you move the mouse to the menu and click on a selection, choices appear.

Tool Bar The tool bar performs some commonly accessed features. It's like other Windows tool bars, in that all you have to do is click on the icon for the specified action to occur. Let's quickly go over the Air Mosaic tool bar icons.

The Tool	Its Name	What You Do with It
Open	Open	Open a document via a URL.
Hotlist	Hotlist	View your Hotlist.
Back	Back	Jump back to the previous page or document in your history list.
Forward	Forward	Jump forward to the next page or document in your history list. (If you're on the last item in the history list you'll stay on that page).
Reload	Reload	Refresh the currently loaded document. (You may need to do this if, for instance, you have a temporary communications problem with the Web server you're connected to.)
Home	Home	Return to the start-up home page.
Find	Find	Find specified text in the current document.

The Tool	Its Name	What You Do with It
Kiosk	Kiosk	Switch from the usual Windows-style window to a full-screen view.
Stop	Stop	Cancel the process of loading an incoming document.
Add	Add	Adds the page you are viewing to your Hotlist.

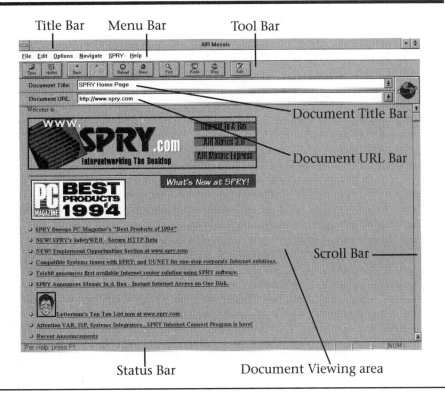

FIGURE 3.2: Here's a pretty typical Air Mosaic window with all its parts labeled so you can see what's what.

You can display the tool bar as Pictures, Text, or Both Pictures & Text. The default is Both Pictures & Text; you may want to change this to free up screen space so the Web documents you view will seem bigger. To change the tool bar's on-screen appearance, select Options ➤Toolbar Style from the menu bar. The Toolbar Style dialog box will appear. Click on the radio button next to the style of your choice, then click on OK.

Document Title Bar Here you'll see the title of the document you are viewing.

Document URL Bar Here you'll see the URL (the Uniform Resource Locator) of the document. We'll get to a discussion of URLs a little later in this chapter.

Document Viewing Area This is the main portion of the screen—it's where you'll see what you came to the Web to see.

Status Bar The status bar is at the bottom of the screen. As you move the cursor about the document viewing area and come across links, the cursor changes into the shape of a hand with one finger pointing and the status bar displays the URL for the link.

Scroll Bars These are just like regular Windows scroll bars: they appear on the side of the viewing area, and possibly at the bottom, when the document is too big to fit in the window. Click on the scroll bars to bring into view whatever's off the screen.

So you want to get rid of all that screen clutter altogether and just click around Web pages unencumbered by tool and menu bars or title and status bars? You can clear away all that stuff so your screen shows only the Web document of the moment. This state is called Kiosk mode. To enter Kiosk mode, click on the Kiosk button on the tool bar, or select Options ➤Kiosk Mode from the menu bar. When you're sick of all that space or you need a tool that's now gone from your screen, you can exit Kiosk mode by pressing either the Escape key or Ctrl-K.

Opening Your First Document

You actually opened your first document when you started Air Mosaic and the home page appeared. But let's dig around a little further and see what else we can open.

Following Hot Links

As we've said before, hypertext is nonlinear. (That means you don't have to follow a straight path from point A to point Z, but rather you can skip around from one place to another to another, back to the first, round to a fourth, etc....) Hypertext has links—*hot links*, they're often called—to other sources of information. You follow these links through a document, or from document to document, or perhaps from server to server, in any way you like as you navigate the Web. (You can think of hypertext as both the text and the links—it's the navigational means by which you traverse the Web.)

How can you tell what is hypertext in a document? Typically, the text on your screen appears highlighted with color and/or underlining, or an image appears there with an added border of color. These qualities all indicate hypertext.

Moving around the World Wide Web via Air Mosaic is a snap, thanks to hyperlinks. It's as easy as a mouse-click on the hyperlink—each hyperlink points to another document, image, sound, etc., and when you click, you jump right to whatever's represented by the item you clicked on.

If we slowed the whole business down and showed you its underpinnings, you'd see that when you click on a hyperlink, Air Mosaic does one of these things:

◆ Gets the document which the link specifies and displays it.

◆ Goes to another location in the current document.

◆ Gets a file such as a sound or image file, and through the use of an external viewer (another piece of software on your PC), plays the sound or displays the image.

◆ Gives you access to another Internet service, such as gopher, FTP, telnet, etc.

If you still have the Air Mosaic home page open, follow a few links between documents by clicking on the home page's hyperlinks. You'll soon see why they call it the Web. Try jumping back and forth a couple of times, too, by clicking on those tools in the tool bar. When you've had enough, just click on the home icon to get back to your start-up home page.

 When you move back to a document that you have already seen, Air Mosaic indicates this to you either by changing the color of the hot link or by replacing the solid underlining with dashes. This is just meant to let you know you've been to that place before.

Opening a Document Using Its URL

Sometimes you're going to want to go straight to the document—you know where it is, and you just want to see it without starting on a home page and skipping through a lot of hot links. Maybe your pal just sent you the URL for the Exploratorium, a really wonderful interactive science museum in San Francisco.

To open a document using its URL:

1. Select File ➤ Open URL from the menu bar. The Open URL dialog box will appear (Figure 3.3).

2. Type the URL of interest in the URL text box. (In our example, **http://www.exploratorium.edu/**.)

3. Click on OK, and Mosaic will find the document for this URL and display it on your screen. (See Figure 3.4.)

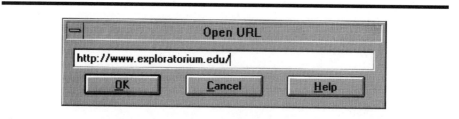

FIGURE 3.3: The Open URL dialog box

URLS Explained Here

Remember that talk about e-mail addresses in Chapter 1? There's a standard addressing scheme with which Mosaic and the Web work, too. It's called the Uniform Resource Locator (URL). The URL pinpoints the locations of documents and other information on the Web so Air Mosaic and other browsers can find the stuff. The structure of a URL may seem complicated at first, but it's really pretty straightforward.

The components of the URL are:

◆ The type of resource

◆ The name of the machine containing the file (the document or information) to be transferred

◆ The full path that locates the file among the directories and subdirectories on the machine

For example, in the URL

```
http://www.ncsa.uiuc.edu/SDG/Software/
WinMosaic/HomePage.html
```

the resource type and transfer protocol are `http` (which, as you know, is HyperText Transfer Protocol), the name of the computer is `www.ncsa.uiuc.edu`, and the path and filename of the item on the computer is `SDG/Software/WinMosaic/HomePage.html`.

To you all this navigation and addressing will be transparent most of the time; Air Mosaic uses the URL embedded in the HTML document to locate the document via hyperlinks behind the scenes.

One thing you should keep in mind, though, is that, unlike e-mail addresses, URLs are case-sensitive (capitalization matters)! This is because lots of Web servers are Unix machines; Unix filenames are longer than DOS filenames and can include uppercase text. So as you use different URLs, keep in mind that case *does* matter.

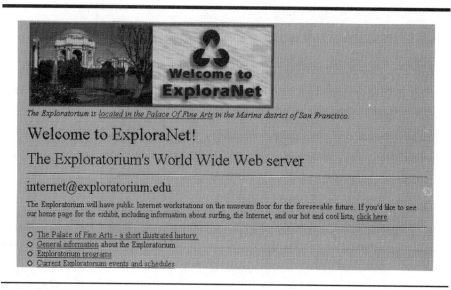

FIGURE 3.4: Here's the Exploratorium's home page. We found it using the URL a friend gave us.

The Web is <u>very</u> BIG. And it changes all the time. From time to time you might have difficulty locating or accessing a document. The original may have been removed by its owner, the machine that holds the document may be unavailable or overworked when you try to access it, or the network path between your machine and the server might be down. If Air Mosaic has been trying for a while to access a document without success, it will display a dialog box saying it just plain cannot locate the document. You can go back to the document that was on screen before you tried making the jump by clicking on OK.

Saving Stuff to Your Local Machine

Let's say you've been skipping around the Internet and looking at a lot of stuff and you found something really nifty you want to hold on to.

 Saving takes up valuable disk space. This means you don't want to save <u>everything</u>. You do want to save things you want to keep for reference or to access quickly in the future.

There are two ways to save a document to your local hard drive. We'll get to those in a second; first, a word or two on naming files in general and hypertext files in particular.

Naming the Files

Most documents you'll want to save don't conform to the standard DOS file-naming conventions. In DOS, a filename can be up to eight characters long, followed by a period and then by an extension of up to three characters. (This is commonly called the 8.3 standard.) The extension often tells you what kind of file it is. An example might be READTHIS.TXT.

Filenames you find on the Web often will be many characters in length and end in longer extensions. This is because they are often created and stored on Unix machines, and their names follow the Unix file-naming system. But you're using Air Mosaic—a *Windows* product, and that means Windows is really doing the saving. If you don't change the filename when you save the file to disk, Windows will do it for you. To meet the 8.3 convention, Windows will truncate the filename, often resulting in something that is not easy to recognize. So we recommend that you always assign your own filename to any file that you save to your local PC by typing the name into the appropriate text box (described in the sections that follow).

One Way to Save Stuff

The first way is the simplest. To save a single document or file to disk:

1. Press the Shift key and hold it down while you click on the hypertext link with the left mouse button. The Save As dialog box will appear (Figure 3.5). This is much like a Save As dialog box you'd see in any other Windows application.

2. In the File Name Text box, type a filename. You'll use the usual DOS file-naming conventions (up to eight characters, then a period followed by a three-letter extension). Use the extension .HTM because this is a hypertext file and that's the extension for hypertext files.

3. Specify the drive and directory if you like, using the Drives pull-down list and the Directories box.

4. Click on OK.

Perhaps this is obvious, but you won't see the document you've saved on screen when you save it. You'll know it's been saved when you check the Directory list and see the filename there.

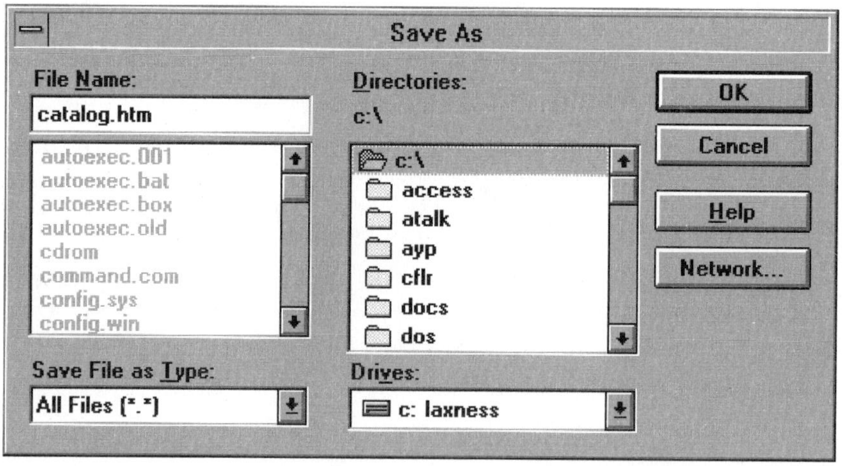

FIGURE 3.5: This is the same Save As dialog box you've seen in other Windows applications.

Another Way to Save Stuff

Let's say you're going to want to save a *lot* of stuff. You can toggle on Air Mosaic's Save option, and basically, every time you view something, it will be saved automatically to your local hard drive.

To use this option:

1. In the Air Mosaic menu bar, select Options ➤ Load to Disk Mode. Pull the menu down one more time to confirm that a check mark appears next to the Load to Disk selection.

2. Now each time you click on a hyperlink the Save As dialog box will appear. In the File Name Text box, type a filename. Use the DOS file-naming conventions (up to eight characters, then a period followed by a three-letter extension), and make the extension .HTM because this is a hypertext file and that's the extension for hypertext files.

3. Specify the drive and directory if you like, using the Drives pull-down list and the Directories box.

4. Click on OK.

To verify that the save was successful, you can check the Directory list to see if the filename is there.

Viewing Documents You've Saved

You can view a document you've saved to your local hard drive by selecting File ➤ Open Local File from Air Mosaic's menu bar. The Open dialog box will appear; again this is a standard Windows dialog box. Select and open the .HTM file of interest by double-clicking on it. By the way, saving a file and then viewing it this way is a lot faster than accessing and viewing it when it's somewhere else in the world; the drawback is that it's no longer dynamic, in that if the owner of the document makes changes, you won't know about it. A really cool aspect of this, though, is that when you view a document that's been saved to your local machine, *the links have been saved with it* and you can just click on those links and start up your Web travels again.

● Jumping Back and Forth While Viewing a Document

The Back and Forward icons on the tool bar provide you with a convenient way to jump back and forth along the hot links you've followed.

Air Mosaic keeps track of the documents you've visited as a history list so you can do this. If you have Air Mosaic running, try clicking on the Back icon to jump backward along the links you've just followed, then click on Forward to jump forward.

There is an end to this—if you jump back to the first document you've viewed in this session, or forward to the last one, you've reached the end of history. You can, as always, create more history—click on another hypertext link to explore further.

At the bottom of many documents you'll find a hot word that says something like Go Back, which, if you click on it, will quickly jump you back to the last document you viewed. It's usually quicker, however, to click on the Back icon on the tool bar to go back.

● You Can Get There from Here in a Snap: Your Hotlist

A big part of managing your Air Mosaic tour of the Web is going to be keeping track of what you found and liked. One way you can revisit what's worthy is to save files to disk, a process we described earlier in this chapter. But you don't always want the stuff on your disk—it takes up valuable disk space. When you stumble across something on the Web that you want easy access to in the future, you should add it to your Hotlist. The Hotlist appears as an option on the File menu.

When you open up the Hotlist, you'll find that Spry has provided you with a handy set of stuff to get you started. We'll go over these in Chapter 4.

Adding Documents to Your Hotlist

When you're viewing a page or document you like so much you want to add it to your Hotlist, click on the Add icon on the toolbar.

The URL for whatever you're so taken with will appear on your Hotlist in the next go-round. It's not the page you'll be saving, however; it's the URL. This means that when you revisit the page you found so interesting, it may have changed. This can be both an advantage, in that you may find even more interesting stuff there next time, and a disadvantage, in that whatever you liked so much the first time might be gone on your next visit.

 Any document you add will appear in the Hotlist category or subcategory you had opened last during this Air Mosaic session. If you have not yet opened a category or subcategory during this session, the document will appear in the top-most category in the list.

Quickly Jumping to Documents on the Hotlist

Any time you're using Air Mosaic, regardless of where you are or what you're viewing, you can go to the Hotlist and jump to whatever's there.

The first time you open the Hotlist, a listing of categories appears. These default Hotlist categories, which we describe in detail in Chapter 4's *What's on the Air Mosaic Hotlist* section, are very good starting points for using the Web. In your later Web sessions, the list will also include any documents you've added to your Hotlist.

Each item in the Hotlist is identified by an icon that shows what type of thing it is. In the first level you'll see one or both of these icons:

 Indicates that this is a category

 Indicates that this is a document

If you double-click on a category, the list expands a level, showing more documents perhaps, and a number of items marked with:

Indicates that this is a subcategory

Using the Hotlist is as convenient as it can be.

1. Select File ➤ Hotlists from the menu bar. The Hotlist dialog box will appear (Figure 3.6).

2. You can just double-click on the title of a document of interest, or you can follow an easy path through the categories: double-click on a category, then on a subcategory (if necessary), and you'll get to a list of documents, any of which you can select by double-clicking on it.

The selected document will open and you'll be on your way.

 You can build a Hotlist with an unlimited number of items, although common sense might suggest that you keep the list shorter, so that "hot" really means <u>hot</u>—that is, so you're able to find the specific item of interest without having to search a long, unwieldy list.

Hotlist Housekeeping

Hotlist housekeeping is a lot like file cabinet organization. Sometimes you'll want to toss out the old unused stuff, add new stuff, and shift things around so they make more sense. You can add new categories and subcategories to your Hotlist; you can also remove items that have outworn their usefulness.

```
                        Hotlists

 SPRY                                    Open/New...
 World Wide Web Search Tools
 Back of the Box                         Add...

                                         Insert...

                                         Remove

                                         Edit...

                                         Export...
 ☐ Put this Hotlist in the menu bar

        Close                    Help
```

FIGURE 3.6: The Hotlist dialog box

Creating New Categories

Each category that appears in your Hotlist actually represents its own file on your hard disk. So when you want to create a new category, you'll actually be creating a new file.

To create a new category:

1. Select File ➤ Hotlists from the menu bar. The Hotlist dialog box (Figure 3.6) will appear.

2. In the dialog box, click on the Open/New button. The Open dialog box (Figure 3.7) will appear. (Don't let this dialog box's name confuse you. We're using it to create a new category.)

3. In the File Name text box, type a filename. This file will hold your category and its contents, so pick a name that's somewhat related to the name you plan for your new category. Note, too, that you're

70

CHAPTER

3

Open Hotlist/Create New Hotlist

File **N**ame:	**D**irectories:	OK
`*.hot`	c:\spry\bin	Cancel

📂 c:\
📂 spry
📂 bin
📁 english

Cancel

Help

☐ **R**ead Only

Network...

List Files of **T**ype: **Dri**ves:

Mosaic Hotlists [*.hot] ▼   c: laxness ▼

FIGURE 3.7: We'll use the Open dialog box to create a new category.

stuck with the DOS file-naming conventions here; limit your file-name to eight characters, and end it with the extension .HOT to indicate to Air Mosaic that it's a Hotlist category file.

In the Open dialog box, you'll see information indicating the drive and directory where the file will be stored. Don't change the drive or directory. The Hotlist files must all be stored on the same drive and in the same directory as Air Mosaic.

4. Having entered the filename for your new category, click on the OK button. The Name This Hotlist dialog box will appear (Figure 3.8).

5. In the dialog box's text box, type a name for your new category. (It can be longer than eight characters, and it can include spaces. No DOS conventions in force here.) Click on the OK button and the dialog box will close.

The Hotlist dialog box will now show your new category in its listing. You may have to scroll down the list of categories to see the new one; it will appear as the last item in the list.

Name this hotlist...

Untitled

| OK | Cancel |

FIGURE 3.8: Type a name for your new category in the Name This Hotlist dialog box's text box.

Creating New Subcategories

Subcategories are not separate files; rather they are part of a category file. You can create your own subcategories within preexisting categories or within categories you create using the directions above. You can even create a subcategory within a subcategory (making a sub-subcategory).

To create a subcategory:

1. Select File ➤ Hotlists from the menu bar. The Hotlist dialog box will appear.
2. Highlight the category or subcategory into which you want to place your new subcategory.
3. Click on the Add button. The Add New dialog box will appear.
4. In the Add New dialog box, click on the word Folder to select it.
5. Click on the OK button. The Add Folder dialog box will appear.
6. In the Add Folder's Title text box, type a name for your new subcategory.
7. Click on the OK button. The Add Folder dialog box will close.

Your new subcategory will now appear in the Hotlist. You can use the Add button on the toolbar to add documents to your subcategory, as described earlier in this chapter.

Removing Items from Your Hotlist

Out with the old and in with the new! You can remove any category, subcategory, or document you wish from your Hotlist, making room for fresher material.

To delete items from your Hotlist:

1. Select File ➤ Hotlists. The Hotlist dialog box will appear.
2. Highlight the category, subcategory, or document you wish to remove from your Hotlist.
3. Click on the Remove button. A dialog box will appear asking you to confirm your action.
4. Click on the OK button.

In the Hotlist dialog box (which will still be visible) the item you deleted will be gone from the listing.

 If you delete a category or subcategory from your Hotlist, anything contained within that category or subcategory will vanish along with it.

Reading and Writing Usenet News with Air Mosaic

Unlike many other forms of Mosaic, Air Mosaic provides you with fully workable access to *Usenet*. Usenet, which some people think *is* the Internet, is a collection of discussion groups, called *newsgroups*, each organized around a specific topic or area of interest. Using Air Mosaic you can read and post *articles* (messages) to those newsgroups that interest you.

Keep in mind the important point that the URLs for newsgroups start with *news:* rather than *http:*. Knowing this handy fact, you can access Usenet news via Air Mosaic Express either by simply clicking on a link that points to a newsgroup, or, if you know the URL (which is just the name of the newsgroup preceded by news:) of a specific newsgroup, by following these easy steps:

1. Select File ➤ Open URL from the Air Mosaic menu bar. The Open URL dialog box will appear.
2. In the text box, type the URL for the newsgroup of interest, for example, **news:comp.os.linux.announce**.

The History Window as Hotlist

You might think of the History window as a pseudo-Hotlist. The History window is a log of every move you make in your Air Mosaic session; each time you launch Air Mosaic, the History window starts empty, then it fills up with a list of your moves as you go along. To see the History window, select Navigate ➤ History from the menu bar. You can highlight anything listed there and then click on Load to go to that item. This makes it possible to use the History window as a kind of short-term Hotlist.

You can also use the History window to retrace your steps. This is more convenient than continuously pressing the Back icon, but it's not terrifically convenient. You have to scroll through the list of places you've been, find the one you want, and click the Load button on the bottom of the window—not as quick as using the Hotlist perhaps, but handy in many circumstances.

The History window will start anew every time you launch Air Mosaic; it also begins anew when you jump back in history by ten moves. In other words, all your moves will appear in the History window *until* you jump back ten moves. If you do so, all the moves after the one you went back to will be thrown away and the History window will start adding to its log the moves that take place from that time forward.

If you change your mind about returning to the past in the History window, simply press Dismiss to close the History window and return to Air Mosaic's document viewing area.

3. Click on the OK button. The Open URL dialog box will close, and in a few seconds a list of news articles (Figure 3.9) will appear.

When you open up a newsgroup, Air Mosaic shows you the titles of the twenty most recent articles in that newsgroup. To see a list of articles that were posted earlier, click on the Earlier articles... link at the top of the page.

Articles in comp.os.linux.announce

Earlier articles...
Post to newsgroup

- "Linux-OS Talk Area" - jeffrey@thompson.itm.org
- "Printing iso-8859-2 text to PostScript via mpage_filter" - Jan Kasprzak (kas@muni.cz)
- "Report from Dec 1 Linux Conference at FedUnix" - cjf@netaxs.com (Chris Fearnley)
- "SVGAFFT release 0.1 alpha made available" - Andrew Veliath (drewvel@ayrton.eideti.com)
- "new shared libjpeg, shared ImageMagick, xv-3.10 and zgv-2.4" - leitner@inf.fu-berlin.de (Felix von Leitner)
- "cdda2wav0.3alpha" - heiko@colossus.escape.de (Heiko Eissfeldt)
- "libg++ 2.6.2.1 is released" - hjl@nynexst.com (H.J. Lu)
- "BCG-game-pack-1.0.bin.ELF.tgz uploaded to sunsite.unc.edu" - umlin000@cc.umanitoba.ca (Zhuo Er Lin)
- "chichot-0.07 Agent Tool/Personal Assistant with Tk Interface." - wieckows@exa.cs.umn.edu (Zbigniew Wieckowski)
- "Chinese Tools 1.3 uploaded to sunsite.unc.edu" - umlin000@cc.umanitoba.ca (Zhuo Er Lin)
- "Emacs 19.28 on sunsite." - stuckey@mrcnext.cso.uiuc.edu (Anthony J. Stuckey)
- "CDROM AZTECH,ORCHID,OKANO,WEARNES" - zimmerma%ntpc34@news.BelWue.DE ()
- "Missing Changes from patches to compile the kernel with elf." - biro@yggdrasil.com (Ross Biro)
- "New ImageMagick binary (sorry for the mess !)" - leitner@inf.fu-berlin.de (Felix von Leitner)
- "Linux a.out DLL support for Khoros 2.0.1 DR" - Wolfram Gloger (wmglo@Dent.MED.Uni-Muenchen.DE)
- "Cygnus makes patches to gcc to work around Pentium divide bug!" - crash@cygnus.com (Jason Molenda)
- "Kernel Patch Change Summary 1.1.70 -) 1.1.71" - Anand Kumria (wildfire@ftoomsh.socs.uts.EDU.AU)
- "PC Week Labs chooses Linux for Top Products" - nelson@crynwr.com (Russell Nelson)
- "CORRECTION to DR Linux Posting- Kernal Hackers Guide is version 0.5 !" - "ACC Corp." (bob@acc-corp.com)
- "X11-QMR Ver 1.4" - ross@wanda.iaccess.za (Ross Linder)

FIGURE 3.9: When you open a newsgroup via Air Mosaic, a list of recently posted ariticles will appear. You can view the contents of any article by clicking on its title in the list.

No matter which technique you use to open a newsgroup, you can look at any of the articles in it by clicking on the title of the article that interests you. When you do this, Air Mosaic will transfer the contents of that article (not the whole newsgroup, for heaven's sake) to your computer and display it on screen (Figure 3.10).

You can add your favorite newsgroups to your Hotlist, just as you would a Web page. When a newsgroup appears in the Hotlist, it will be preceded by the word Newsgroup. You can just double-click on the name of a newsgroup in the Hotlist to fire up your fave rave.

Linux-OS Talk Area

Followup to message

jeffrey@thompson.ttm.org
27 Dec 1994 15:33:54 +0200
?

○ Newsgroups: comp.os.linux.announce

```
If you're excited about Linux OS like I am, and have some questions
about it, wouldn't it be great if you could go somewhere on the
internet and ask a question?  I've setup a 'Linux-OS Talk Area' in the
Diversity University (DU) MOO/MUD.  It's a place where people can talk
about Linux!

I'm encouraging everyone I know to use Linux.

To get there do this:

   telnet moo.du.org 8888                (don't forget 8888)
   connect guest
   @go #11848
   @quit (to exit)
```

FIGURE 3.10:   We opened up an article titled Linux-OS Talk Area by clicking on its title; here's what we saw in the article.

To post new articles to a newsgroup using Air Mosaic, just click on the Post to newsgroup link that appears near the top of a news window. A dialog box will appear asking for some information: your name and e-mail address (these will be filled in automatically), the newsgroup to post the article to, the subject of the article, keywords (to help others who are searching for articles on specific topics to find yours), and the text of the article. In Figure 3.11, you can see the dialog box with all this stuff filled in. Once you have filled in all the information, click on the Send button to send the message off. A dialog box will soon appear saying that your message was posted successfully. (Note, however, that it may take minutes or even *hours* for your article to appear in the newsgroup—it all depends on the flow of traffic.)

Air Mosaic News

Sender:	dat@netcom.com
Newsgroup	comp.os.linux.announce
Subject:	New Book on Linux
Keywords:	book linux
Content-type:	text/plain

Enter the message body:

We've just about finished our book on Linux. It includes lots of information on installing and using this full-featured Unix clone; also included is a CD that has on it Linux (the Slackware distribution), the source code, and the Linux Documentation Project's documents.

Send   Cancel

FIGURE 3.11:   Posting a Usenet article is a snap with Air Mosaic.

Newsgroups and articles will appear in the History window, just as Web pages do. There, newsgroups will show up as a URL starting with news:, articles appear starting with news: but ending with the article's unique ID (identifier)—an odd-looking combination of letters and numbers that will include an @ sign. Remember, you can double-click on anything in the History window to jump to that item.

Do You Need Help?

For technical support, contact Spry at (206) 447-0958 Monday through Friday between 8 a.m. and 5 p.m. (Pacific standard time). For general information or billing questions, contact Spry at (206) 447-0300, also during business hours, or at (800) SPRYNET.
Spry's URL is `http://www.spry.com`.

Quitting Air Mosaic

You can quit Air Mosaic any ol' time—even when the world icon is animated. To leave Air Mosaic:

1. If the world icon is animated, click on the Stop button on the tool bar. This will cancel whatever Air Mosaic is trying to do at the moment. (If the world icon is not animated, skip this step.)

2. To actually quit the program, double-click on the control button in the upper-left corner of the screen.

   or

   Choose File ➤ Exit from the menu bar.

This will quit you out of Air Mosaic and break the Internet connection, leaving you with a familiar view of your Windows desktop.

Now, with your basic skills in place for navigating the Web via Air Mosaic, let's turn our attention to some great starting points and then to cool places you can visit.

Good and Useful Starting Points

You can jump into the Web from any of what seem like zillions of places. This is part of its attraction, but it can be overwhelming when you start your exploration. When you're following links from one document to another document, it's also easy to forget how you got to a particular resource gold mine. You may find it difficult to retrace your steps later on.

Fortunately, there are some great comprehensive starting points on the Web that can really help get you going, and Air Mosaic provides several tools that can help you get started and even retrace your electronic trail. By the end of this chapter you should have a pretty good line on how and where to jump in. You'll also know how to use Air Mosaic's features to keep the places you've been (and those you need to get back to quickly) just a mouse-click away.

 Inside the front cover of this book you'll find a convenient list of starting places that includes those we discuss in this chapter and a few more.

The Big Picture

In Chapter 3 we showed you how to start Air Mosaic and navigate around. When you launch Air Mosaic you'll see the start-up home page. The first time you start Air Mosaic, that will be the default home page. Later, if you like, you can change things to display a different home page on startup. The default home page is not a bad place to start—we'll look a little more closely at what it has to offer in a second. There are other good starting places, too, however, so in this chapter we'll also look at:

♦ Starting Points for Internet Exploration

♦ Information by Subject

♦ Data Sources by Service

♦ Web Servers Directory

♦ NCSA Mosaic What's New Document

♦ The Air Mosaic default Hotlist as a point of departure

These are all places you can get to from the Air Mosaic home page. Before we look into these in detail, let's go over some general information about home pages.

What Is a Home Page, Really?

You can look at this in a couple of ways. To you, the user, the home page is a starting point for exploring the World Wide Web. A home page might be seen as kind of a "main menu." This analogy breaks down a bit because the Web is neither hierarchical nor linear and Mosaic is by no means menu-driven, but a home page does outline your options for you—at least the options for moving along the links from the home page to other points of interest on the Web, as imagined by the publisher of this particular home page. To whomever publishes it, the home page is part advertisement, part directory, and part "reference librarian." Publishers of a home page have to think through its construction completely to make it clear what the page is about and what can be found there.

In reality, a home page is a hypertext document with links to other points on the Web. The start-up home page, the one that is automatically loaded each time you launch Air Mosaic, should be one that helps you get going. It may be the default start-up home page or one that is specialized to your interests. You can even set it up so Air Mosaic won't access and display a home page, though why you'd want to start out without the benefit of a good start-up home page is beyond us.

 A whole toolkit of frequently accessed home pages is at your disposal under Air Mosaic's preconfigured Hotlist. Click on the Hotlist icon on the tool bar and you can see which starting points Spry (the distributor of Air Mosaic) currently recommends. To select one, just double-click on its name in the list.

Changing Your Start-Up Home Page

For new users and experienced users whose purposes are fairly general, the default start-up home page (the one that appears when you first launch Air Mosaic) or another of those we describe in this chapter might be best. For those with specialized interests, a specific home page geared to those interests might be better. Let's say, for example, that you're doing a long-term research project on the subject of language and thought. You know what you want—none of this general stuff. For the duration of your project, you might set your start-up home page to the one published by Stanford University's Linguistics Department. That way, each time you launch Air Mosaic, you'll immediately see the Stanford Linguistics Department's home page and you can begin your research from that point. When you've finished that project and begin another—this time writing environmental assessment reports for a large government contractor—you instead use the U.S. Geological Survey's home page as your start-up page.

To speed up your Web travels you might want to choose as your start-up home page one that is tailored to your interests. This is getting easier to do, with the Web's rate of growth—perhaps you work for a company that has its own home page. Remember: you can actually get anywhere on the Web from almost anywhere else on the Web, so it makes sense to make your start-up home page as convenient for you as possible. You can even construct your own custom home page using HTML, as you'll see in Chapter 7.

To change your start-up home page you'll use Air Mosaic's configuration dialog box—this is the dialog box from which you can change many facets of how Air Mosaic is set up on your machine.

Here are the steps for changing your home page:

1. With Air Mosaic running, select Options ➤ Configuration from the menu bar. The Configuration dialog box will appear.

2. In the dialog box, you'll find a section labeled *Home Page*, and in that, a text box labeled *URL*. The URL for the home page currently slated for display at startup will appear in the text box (Figure 4.1). Highlight that URL and type in its place the URL for the home page you want.

3. Click on the OK button. The Configuration dialog box will close and the Air Mosaic window will appear.

Now when you start Air Mosaic again, you should see the home page you just designated as your start-up page.

Let's say you have some reason for not wanting to see any home page at all when you launch Air Mosaic. The steps you'll follow to do this are very similar to those for changing the start-up home page:

1. With Air Mosaic running, select Options ➤ Configuration from the menu bar. The Configuration dialog box will appear.

2. In the box area labeled *Home Page*, find *Load automatically at startup* and click on its check box.

Configuration

☒ Show Toolbar   ☒ Autoload inline images
☒ Show Status Bar   ☒ Show URL in Status Bar
☒ Show Document Title   ☒ Underline hyperlinks
☒ Show Document URL   ☒ Animate logo
☐ Save last window position   ☐ Use 8-bit Sound

When loading images, redraw every 1.5 seconds.

Home Page

URL: http://www.spry.com/mbox/

☒ Load automatically at startup

Email Address: anonymous@interserv.com
SMTP Server: relay.interserv.com
News Server: news.spry.com

Cached Documents: 10   Documents in dropdown: 5

Viewers...   Link Color...   Fonts...   Proxy Servers...

OK   Cancel   Help

FIGURE 4.1: Type in the URL for the home page you want to appear at startup.

3. Now click on the OK button. The Configuration dialog box will close and the Air Mosaic window will appear.

What could be easier? Now when you launch Air Mosaic again, you should see absolutely no home page at startup. Instead you'll see an empty document window.

Just because you've changed your start-up home page or arranged for none to appear at startup doesn't mean you can't access the original home page whenever you want. It's available with the URL `http://www.spry.com/mbox`. In addition, all of Spry's home pages appear in your Hotlist, as you'll discover later in this chapter.

Now let's take a look at some good all-purpose home pages, starting with the default start-up home page you've heard so much about.

The Default Start-Up Home Page

When you launch Air Mosaic, you'll see the default start-up home page — probably the Mosaic in a Box home page. (This is because Spry Mosaic, the software that comes with this book, is the licensed, functional equivalent of Mosaic in a Box). The Web is an ever-changing environment, and the folks at Sybex and Spry will want you to keep up with the latest trends, so this home page is bound to be dynamic. Look here for starting points of all sorts, including, at this writing, links to:

HotLand A subject-oriented guide to resources on the Web, ranging from Computers to Kids to News & Magazines, Personal Finance, Sports, and more. Click on any of the links shown in HotLand to display a page filled with links to Web resources on that topic.

User Tips A link to a bigger set of links connecting you to all sorts of juicy information about Air Mosaic. Follow the links and you'll find tips, technical support, and a feedback form to let Spry know what you think about the product.

Add-Ons A link to a page that describes add-on products Spry is marketing to work in conjunction with the software you have.

Remember, this page is bound to change. Whatever you find in place of what we've described is sure to be useful and even entertaining. Check it out.

NCSA Mosaic for Microsoft Windows Home Page

NCSA, the original creator of Mosaic, maintains a home page filled with information about its software, NCSA Mosaic.

This is a very good place to visit, in that it provides plenty of information about Mosaic itself. (Remember, Air Mosaic is an enhanced form of NCSA Mosaic.) When a new version of NCSA Mosaic is available, an announcement will be posted here to tell you so (see Figure 4.2). There are also links here to other software you might want to use with Air Mosaic—for example, those external viewers we mention in Chapter 2 and tell you how to use in Chapter 8. The NCSA Mosaic for Microsoft Windows home page also talks a lot about how the Web was developed and so on.

On the other hand, this is *such* a fountain of basic information that pretty much everyone starts here, and that's not good. This is a heavy traffic area, so much so that Mosaic's developers at NCSA/UIUC would like you to use some other start-up home page to take the weight off this one. If you make up your mind to change your start-up home page from the default start-up home page to another, this is obviously *not* your best bet.

Let's look at what makes this home page so useful in your Web travels.

Downloading Viewers and Other Software

When the folks who developed NCSA Mosaic have new versions available, an announcement is posted on the NCSA Mosaic for Microsoft Windows

86

CHAPTER

4

Good and Useful Starting Points

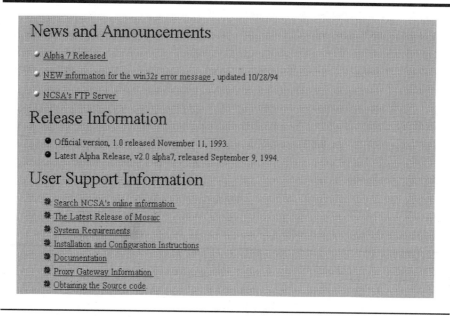

FIGURE 4.2: A new version of NCSA Mosaic is available!

home page. Likewise, when new viewers become available for use with Mosaic, an announcement is posted. In fact, the people at NCSA will tell you about pretty much whatever they find that they think you might want, as long as they think it's good stuff. Your option, then, is to take advantage of this opportunity by downloading whatever you think you can use. (See *Mosaic for Microsoft Windows and NCSA Mosaic: A Tale of Two Home Pages* later in this chapter.)

When you're looking over the NCSA Mosaic for Microsoft Windows home page and you see an announcement telling you about new software, you'll be told in the announcement more or less how to get the software. Here are two possible scenarios:

◆ The announcement will say something like "…you can get it here:" and will be followed by a blue, underlined word. This indicates that the link is to the software file itself.

◆ The announcement will say something like "…you can get it from *X-Y-Z* place" and *X-Y-Z* will be blue and underlined. This indicates that the link is to wherever the software file is located.

In either case, all you have to do is click on the link. If the link is to the software file itself, the Save As dialog box will appear, allowing you to save the file to your local machine. If the link is not directly to the software but rather to its location, some sort of page will appear, probably telling you about the software; in turn, that page will have a link for you to click on, and when you do, the Save As dialog box will appear.

Saving software files with the Save As dialog box is a very straightforward Windows operation; you probably won't have to (or even want to) rename the files but you may want to specify the drive and directory you want them to land in.

Downloading software is a lot like saving files to your local machine, which we described in detail in Chapter 3.

Often you'll find that the software files you download from the Web are *zipped*—they've been compressed with a utility like PKZip or LHarc—which you'll know because the filename ends in either .ZIP (for PKZip) or .LZH (for LHarc).

Compressed Files

Files are zipped (*compressed, shrunk,* or *compacted*) to make them smaller, so they can be transmitted more quickly. Compressed files often can be $1/2$ the size of the original file; some files can be compressed to as little as $1/20$ their original size. If a file has been compressed, you'll need a companion program to uncompress the file. PKZip/PKUnzip are available commercially; LHarc is downloadable freeware. Other compression/decompression programs are also available—some emulate or are compatible with their commercially available cousins. (Zip/Unzip, for example, will compress and uncompress PKZip files.)

What's Out There?

You can find out everything you ever wanted to know about compression from the FAQ (frequently asked questions) list at the URL `http://www.cis.ohio-state.edu/hypertext/faq/usenet/compression-faq/top.html`.

NCSA Mosaic for Microsoft Windows and NCSA Mosaic: A Tale of Two Home Pages

The NCSA Mosaic for Microsoft Windows home page is different from the NCSA Mosaic home page. (They're also both different from the Mosaic in a Box home page, but that's a different story.) If you want information about NCSA Mosaic for Microsoft Windows—the application, new features, bug fixes and enhancements—you'll find it in the NCSA Mosaic for Microsoft Windows home page. The NCSA Mosaic home page was the original default home page, covering not just the Windows product but Mac and Unix, too. When traffic became overwhelming a split was deemed necessary and was carried out.

You'll know which of these home pages is which not only by the difference in content, but by the URL. The NCSA Mosaic for Windows Home Page, which has links to information specific to Mosaic for Windows, has this URL:

```
http://www.ncsa.uiuc.edu/SDG/Software/
WinMosaic/HomePage.html
```

The NCSA Mosaic home page—which contains stuff like general information about the Web, hyperlinks to catalogs, indexes of information that's available by subject—has as its URL:

```
http://www.ncsa.uiuc.edu/SDG/Software/
Mosaic/NCSAMosaicHome.html
```

Check them both out for a more well-rounded view of Mosaic in all its various incarnations.

Other Especially Good Starting Points

As we've mentioned, changing your start-up home page from the default to another one can speed up operations by giving you access to a wide range of resources. Let's take a look at some likely candidates.

NCSA's Starting Points for Internet Exploration

NCSA's Starting Points for Internet Exploration is a document that includes links to information about the Web and Mosaic. (Figure 4.3 shows you this document.) Near the top of the page is a very useful list where links appear for:

◆ Data Sources by Service

◆ Information by Subject

◆ Web News

◆ Web Servers Directory

This is a handy all-purpose set of links to services new Web users will find helpful. Each of these four items is, in fact, another candidate for your start-up home page; let's take a closer look at them one by one.

What's Out There?

The URL for Starting Points for Internet Exploration is
`http://www.ncsa.uiuc.edu/SDG/Software/Mosaic/`
`StartingPoints/NetworkStartingPoints.html`.

Starting Points for Internet Exploration

This document contains hyperlinks to many common Internet-based information resources.

If you are new to NCSA Mosaic, the Mosaic demo document will allow you to explore Mosaic's hypermedia capabilities; this document focuses on Internet resources in general, including several different types of information systems that do not have intrinsic hypermedia capabilities.

Disclaimer: NCSA has no control over any of the resources referenced by this document. Some or all of these resources may be unavailable at any time. This is a random sampling of Internet resources and makes no claim to be general or comprehensive.

- Web Overview: An overview of the World Wide Web, a distributed hypermedia system developed at CERN in Switzerland. NCSA Mosaic is a World Wide Web *client* with additional features.
- Web Project: An overview of the World Wide Web project, headed by Tim Berners-Lee at CERN.
- Other Web Documents:
  - Data Sources By Service: A listing of data sources within the World Wide Web, organized by information service (Gopher, WAIS, etc.).
  - Information By Subject: A listing of data sources within the World Wide Web, organized by topic and subtopic.
  - Web News: The latest World Wide Web news bulletin.
  - Web Servers Directory: The central listing of known World Wide Web servers. Servers not yet registered with this list may be noted in the Mosaic What's New list.
- InterNIC InfoGuide : A Web server run by the InterNIC; this is a good place to find general Internet-related information.
- NCSA Mosaic Home Page: The document NCSA Mosaic accesses upon startup by default; this document tells you what the latest released version of NCSA Mosaic is at any given time.
- NCSA Mosaic Demo Page: A self-guided tour of the hypermedia capabilities of NCSA Mosaic.
- NCSA Mosaic "What's New" Page: A day-by-day listing of new information resources on the Internet available through

FIGURE 4.3: The NCSA's Starting Points for Internet Exploration document is a good place to start.

Data Sources by Service

Another useful way to view of all the information on the Web is by service—that is, FTP, gopher, and WAIS, in addition to HTTP. If you know *where* you might find whatever you're looking for—say, if you know it's on an FTP server at UC Santa Barbara—it makes more sense to look for the information organized by the *type of server* rather than by the topic.

You can check out the services listing by following these steps:

1. Select File ➤ Open URL from the menu bar. The Open URL dialog box will appear.

2. In the Open URL dialog box's text box, type the URL

http://info.cern.ch/hypertext/DataSources/ByAccess.html

3. A document will appear with hypertext links to additional listings for each service type:

◆ World Wide Web servers

◆ WAIS servers

◆ Network News

◆ Gopher

◆ Telnet access

Click on the service type of interest.

4. A detailed listing of servers of that type will appear. Click on the specific server you're looking for; a connection will be established to that server and you can then find what you're seeking. (You started out knowing what and where it was, remember?)

Information by Subject

To get a subject-oriented list of the information that's available, you can select File ➤ Open URL from the menu bar, and in the Open URL dialog box's text box, type the URL **http://info.cern.ch/hypertext/DataSources/bySubject/Overview.html**. The World Wide Web Virtual Library will appear (Figure 4.4). You can click on any category in the Virtual Library to see a list of resources for that category. If you have an idea of which topic you want to explore, here's where to start.

What's Out There?

The URL for the World Wide Web Virtual Library: Subject Catalogue page is `http://info.cern.ch/hypertext/DataSources/bySubject/Overview.html`.

The WWW Virtual Library

This is a distributed subject catalogue. See <u>Summary</u>, and <u>Index</u>. See also arrangement by <u>service type</u> , and <u>other subject catalogues of network information</u>.

Mail to <u>maintainers</u> of the specified subject or www-request@info.cern.ch to add pointers to this list, or if you would <u>like to contribute to administration of a subject area</u>.

See also <u>how to put your data on the web</u>. All items starting with ! are *NEW!* (or newly maintained).

<u>Aboriginal Studies</u>
This document keeps track of leading information facilities in the field of Australian Aboriginal studies as well as the Indigenous Peoples studies.
<u>Aeronautics and Aeronautical Engineering</u>
<u>Agriculture</u>
<u>Anthropology</u>
<u>Applied Linguistics</u>
<u>Archaeology</u>
<u>Architecture</u>
<u>Art</u>
<u>Asian Studies</u>
<u>Astronomy and Astrophysics</u>
<u>Aviation</u>
<u>Bio Sciences</u>
<u>Chemistry</u>

FIGURE 4.4: Click on the Information by Subject link in the Starting Points for Internet Exploration document to open up the World Wide Web Virtual Library: Subject Catalog document.

For example, if you're interested in geology, click on Earth Sciences; after the Air Mosaic world becomes animated, the Earth Sciences listing will be displayed (Figure 4.5). You can make further choices from there—for example, you can go to the Geological Survey of Finland, to the USGS (Figure 4.6), or to MIT's Earth Sciences Department, just to name a few.

What's Out There?

You can retrieve the Earth Sciences list with the URL http://www.geo.ucalgary.ca/VL-EarthSciences.html. The URL for the United States Geological Survey's home page is http://www.usgs.gov.

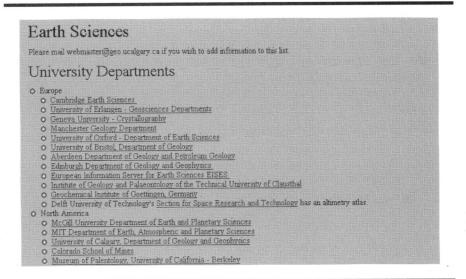

FIGURE 4.5: The Earth Sciences list

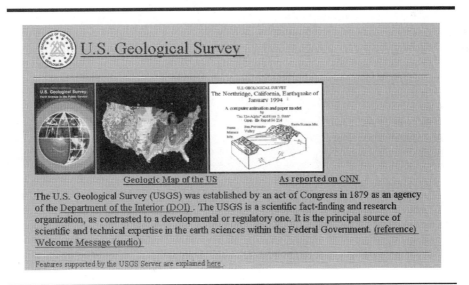

FIGURE 4.6: The USGS home page

Web Servers Directory

The Web, as we've said, is a global network. To explore the Web's branches in other countries, you can use the Web Servers Directory. To access it, select File ➤ Open URL from the menu bar, and in the Open URL dialog box's text box, type the URL **http://info.cern.ch/hypertext/ DataSources/WWW/Servers.html**. The World Wide Web Servers: Summary document will appear. Here you'll find a list of known Web servers around the world, categorized by geographical areas:

◆ Africa

◆ Asia

◆ Australia and Oceania

◆ Central America

◆ Europe

◆ Middle East

◆ North America

◆ South America

The continents with the most Web servers—Asia and North America—are further categorized by country. What's this good for? Well, let's say you're interested in finding out the name of the head of the Computer Science Department at the University of Sydney. This is just the sort of information you're more likely to find on a server in Australia than anywhere else; why not start your search in the right country?

What's Out There?

The Web Servers Directory's URL is `http://info.cern.ch/ hypertext/DataSources/WWW/Servers.html`.

For a more graphical approach than the list offers, click on <u>clickable</u> <u>world</u> <u>map</u> and you'll get a view like that shown in Figure 4.7.

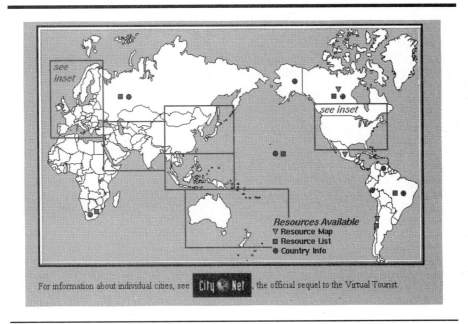

For information about individual cities, see **City Net**, the official sequel to the Virtual Tourist.

FIGURE 4.7: Click on a continent to start tracking down Web servers located there.

NCSA Mosaic What's New Document

The Web is a happening place—new Web servers come online every month. To find out what's new any ol' time, check out the NCSA Mosaic What's New page. When schools, companies, or individuals set up new HTTP servers they send announcements to NCSA with basic information about their server. This information gets linked to the What's New page and a link is born—that is to say, the informational listings on the What's New page are (what else?) hyperlinks to the respective new server.

You can access the What's New page through various hypertext links on a variety of pages throughout the Web. You can also go to the page from the Starting Points menu; just select File ➤ Open URL from the menu bar and, in the Open URL dialog box's text box, type the URL **http://www.ncsa. uiuc.edu/SDG/Software/Mosaic/Docs/whats-new.html**. The What's New listing will appear. The length of this listing at any given time depends on how many Web sites have been announced that month.

The NCSA Mosaic's What's New document is usually quite long. It may take a good long while to transfer it to your computer; but the information it contains is plenty useful and well worth the wait.

What's Out There?

The URL for the NCSA Mosaic's What's New page is http//www .ncsa.uiuc.edu/SDG/Software/Mosaic/Docs/whats-new.html.

The Air Mosaic Hotlist as Point of Departure

The Air Mosaic Hotlist is not just a place where you can store a list of home pages for revisiting, it's also great for getting you started. That's because the Air Mosaic Hotlist starts out with a default list of hot starting places.

Hotlist items can be selected at any time. If you've been following links hither and yon and then decide to pursue a completely new line of exploration, you can select any of the items in the Hotlist. Just click on the Hotlist icon on the toolbar and when the Hotlist dialog box appears, double-click on the item of interest to zoom right to it.

We talked about how to use the Hotlist and how to add items to it in Chapter 3; here we're going to look at the default Air Mosaic Hotlist as a pointer for the next leg of your Web travels.

What's on the Air Mosaic Hotlist

Air Mosaic's default Hotlist is arranged in a series of categories to make finding an area of interest easier. Let's take a quick look at some points of interest among the categories on the Hotlist:

◆ Spry: providing quick access to pages and pages of information about Spry, its doings, and its products

◆ WWW Searching Tools: providing quick access to pages about spiders, crawlers, worms, and other search tools

◆ Back of the Box: providing quick access to even more pages filled with opportunities for shopping and leisure activities

In a general sense, when you double-click on any of these categories, either a list of subcategories or of documents will appear. (If the subcategories appear, you'll again double-click on the area of your interest to get to the list of documents.) In the list of documents, double-click on the one you want to view, and you'll be on your way.

The documents in the Air Mosaic Hotlist, like everything on the Web, are subject to change. We looked at documents via the default Hotlist three times and they were different every time. You may even find somewhat different categories or subcategories than we did.

Now What?

With the Air Mosaic basics under your belt, let's take a wider look at what's available on the World Wide Web. In Chapter 5, we're going to have a look at some sites so hot they sizzle.

Spots on the Web You Won't Want to Miss

Those home pages we talked about in Chapter 4 are great places to get going in your Web exploration, but they sure aren't the end all and be all. Browsing the Web is what Air Mosaic's all about, and browsing is all about happening across the unexpected. As we've said, the Web changes every day; you'll find things we've never dreamed of in your own Web travels. Here to get you started are some hip, happening, and downright amazing things we found on the Web when we were just looking around.

Some Real Roadmarkers

Along the Infobahn, there are many places you'll want to visit. Let's start our survey by looking at what's "best," what's new, and what-makes-it-easy-to-find-what-you-want.

The Best of the Web

Here you'll find hyperlinks to winners of the annual *Best of the World Wide Web* competition, which was spawned at the International World Wide Web Conference in Geneva in May 1994. The winners are selected during a two-month period of open nominations followed by a two-week period of open voting. More than 5,000 votes were cast to select the first year's winners. The point of the contest—and the point of displaying the winners on this server—is to highlight the Web's potential to new users and to information providers. The *Best of the World Wide Web* competition shows what can be done with the Web's underlying technology: the HyperText Markup Language (HTML) and the HyperText Transport Protocol (HTTP).

What's Out There?

You can see winners of the *Best of the World Wide Web* competition through the URL `http://wings.buffalo.edu/contest/`.

The Best of the Web page is a good place to begin exploring the Web. Winners are organized into categories—General, Application, and Technical—within which these awards are given:

◆ Best Overall Site

◆ World Wide Web Hall of Fame

◆ Best Campus-Wide Information System

◆ Best Commercial Service

◆ Best Educational Service

◆ Best Entertainment Site

◆ Best Professional Service

◆ Best Navigational Aid

◆ Most Important Service Concept

- ◆ Best Document Design
- ◆ Best Use of Interaction
- ◆ Best Use of Multiple Media
- ◆ Most Technical Merit

Some of the winners are included in this book—for example, the Xerox PARC Map Viewer we talk about later in this chapter was the *Most Technical Merit* winner in 1994. In Figure 5.1 you can see another winner, the World Wide Web Sports Information Service. Be sure to check out the Best of the Web; you can use the current winners as handy starting points for your Web travels.

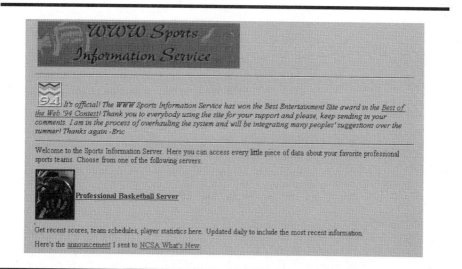

FIGURE 5.1: World Wide Web Sports Information Service provides information about professional basketball and football.

What's New with NCSA Mosaic

We talked about the What's New document briefly in Chapter 4, but it's worth another mention here. Often touted as "The Most Frequently Visited" place on the Web, this dynamic document covers recent changes

and additions to the Web. When new information providers go online, they can submit an announcement to the Keepers of this Page. With the appropriate reference in place in the form of a hyperlink, the new material is accessible from this list simply by clicking on the hyperlinked name in the listing.

What's Out There?

The What's New page is a great place to see the range of material becoming available on the Web. The URL is `http://www.ncsa.uiuc.edu /SDG/Software/Mosaic/Docs/whats-new.html`.

New information providers can submit announcements to the keepers of What's New via the URL `http://WWW.ncsa.uiuc.edu/SDG/ Software/Mosaic/Docs/submit-to-whats-new.html`.

The entire archive of World Wide Web What's New pages is searchable. See Chapter 6 for more information about this resource and how to use it.

The World Wide Web Worm

As you know because you've read Chapter 2, there are Web wanderers, robots, and other automated processes scurrying through the Web to document the numerous Web sites available. The most useful of these is probably the World Wide Web Worm (Figure 5.2). Because the Worm (WWWW) creates an indexed database, and because Air Mosaic provides a way for you to query data through its *forms* mechanism (see Chapter 3), you can send a request to the Worm and it will search the Web all over the world to find out whatever you've requested.

What's Out There?

Find out about the Worm and set it into motion through the URL `http://www.cs.colorado.edu/home/mcbryan/WWWW.html`.

There is one caveat here: the Worm is another overworked resource, and because of this it's sometimes unable to return the listing you want. See Chapter 6 for more on the World Wide Web Worm, including tips for getting the most from it.

Search Operations:

A URL is the address of any multimedia resource on the WWW. A URL may point to an HTML file, a GIF image, an MPEG movie, an AU sound file and so on.

A WWW document page, written in HTML, consists of text and images interspersed with *citations* (also called *anchors*). Each citation appears highlighted (color+underline) in WWW browsers. Clicking on one causes the cited URL to be retrieved and displayed.

The WWW Worm provides a way to locate documents and citations. A URL must be cited in some WWW document page in order to be known to WWWW. Additionaly we regard the (required) Title of a WWW document as implicitly a citation for that document.

Each Citation of a URL is cross-referenced with the document citing it. Since any one URL may be cited in many different documents, individual items may appear multiple times in the list.

WWWW uses the UNIX egrep program to perform searches - it therefore uses egrep regular expressions (man egrep) to create fancy search strings. This is awkward but can also be powerful.

Select:
1. Search only in Titles of citing documents
2. Search only in Names of citing documents
3. Search all Citation Hypertext
4. Search all Names of Cited URL's

Keywords: Xanadu

[Start Search]

FIGURE 5.2: The World Wide Web Worm will help you search the Web efficiently.

Blinded by Science

The Web, and in fact the Internet, started as a research tool, though of course it's grown into much more than that. You can see the effects of these beginnings, though, in the wide range of information on the World Wide Web about everything from nuclear physics to genetic engineering to cancer research to...well, you get the idea. Here's a sampling of some Web servers that are chock full o' fascinating and useful data.

The Exploratorium

Here's a real beauty. The Exploratorium is a hands-on, interactive science museum in San Francisco. To call it a museum, though, is a *bit* misleading—

it's a really FUN place for the whole family. The only problem is that if you live outside the San Francisco Bay Area, it may be difficult to get there. No longer. The Exploratorium, which has been on the Internet for a while now (it *is* a science and technology showplace, after all) now has its very own Web server! Much of the fun (and educational) experience you'd go to the Exploratorium for is now not only online, but also graphical and interactive, in the true Exploratorium spirit (Figure 5.3).

Once you've accessed the Exploratorium's home page, you can click on the <u>Digital Library</u> and then select from a page of offerings ranging from photos of current exhibits to actual interactive versions of electronic exhibits and even (if you have the right sound drivers) a sample of the Doppler effect (you know—how a train sounds as it passes you).

What's Out There?

The Exploratorium experience can be yours through the URL `http://www.exploratorium.edu/`.

MIT SIPB Home Page

Forage for days at the MIT SIPB home page (Figure 5.4), with links to just-about-everywhere-else on the Web, all *very* well organized and easy to access. After all—where better to look into science and technology than that granddaddy of science and technology academia, the Massachusetts Institute of *Technology*?

What's Out There?

The MIT SIPB home page, a real doozie, is available at the URL `http://www.mit.edu:8001`.

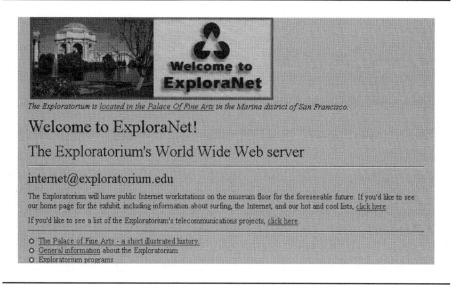

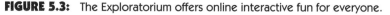

FIGURE 5.3: The Exploratorium offers online interactive fun for everyone.

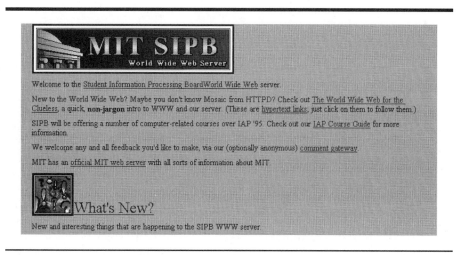

FIGURE 5.4: A home page for that granddaddy of science and technology, MIT

Here you'll also find the latest version of PGP (Pretty Good Privacy), a free public-key encryption mechanism for noncommercial use. You'll also find a hyperlink to a great listing of online resources for women—women in computer science and engineering, women in academia and industry, gender and sexuality, women's studies programs and women's centers (click on Interesting Documents and then click on "A collection of writings and resources on women in computer science and engineering, women on the Net, women's studies, etc.").

Back at the MIT SIPB home page, click on Other Information Servers at MIT to display the More Neat Servers document. You'll find links to pages, providing information about MIT departments, admissions, administration, and other such issues. Scroll further down the page to the MIT Laboratories heading. This is lab-coat city, with links to:

◆ The MIT Laboratory for Nuclear Science

◆ The MIT Microwave Subnode of NASA's Planetary Data System, a subsidiary of the Geosciences node of NASA's Planetary Data System

◆ The MIT Earth Resources Laboratory

◆ The MIT Research Laboratory for Electronics

◆ The MIT Artificial Intelligence Laboratory

◆ The MIT Laboratory for Computer Science, which among several other ventures, has joined forces with CERN in guiding the future direction of the World Wide Web

◆ The MIT Microsystems Technology Laboratories

◆ The MIT Weather Radar Laboratory

◆ The MIT Computational Aerospace Sciences Laboratory

◆ The MIT Plasma Fusion Center

◆ The MIT/Whitehead Center for Genome Research

Theses, general information about the research centers, and links to additional subgroups are all available by following links within a specific laboratory area.

What's Out There?

The URL for direct access to the MIT Microwave Subnode of NASA's Planetary Data System is `http://delcano.mit.edu/`. Among other things, pictures of the Shoemaker-Levy comet are available here.

MIT Media Lab

The MIT Media Lab is widely known as a happening place in the field of technology, particularly regarding human interaction with technology. If you want to learn about current research in *collaborative interface agents*—semi-intelligent systems that will help you with computer-based tasks—check out the Autonomous Agents Group on the MIT Media Lab's home page. Details of several of the Lab's ongoing research projects are available from there, including complete papers.

What's Out There?

You'll get direct access to the MIT Media Lab through the URL `http://debussy.media.mit.edu`.

Mars Atlas Home Page

Cybernauts who are really frustrated astronauts can get vicarious thrills looking at Viking Orbiter shots of Mars (Figure 5.5). The Mars Atlas home page gives you entrée to a browsable, zoomable, and scrollable Mars atlas, providing access to literally thousands of high-resolution Viking Orbiter images.

You can start your search through the Mars atlas in one of three ways:

◆ From a small (600x300-pixel) map

◆ From a larger (1440x720-pixel), more detailed map

◆ From a list of topographical features—mountain, ridge, canyon, and so on

What's Out There?

Your astronaut's eye view of Mars can be found at the URL `http://fi-www.arc.nasa.gov/fia/projects/bayes-group/Atlas/Mars/`.

Just one caveat: the file's big maps are *really big*. For this gizmo to really work, you're going to have to wait a while for the maps to be transferred. (Go get coffee.)

Academia is Only Mouse-Clicks Away

Several other worthwhile university home pages are readily available. One that's especially interesting is the home page for the ANU (Australian National University) Bioninformatics Facility, which is part of ANU's Centre for Molecular Structure and Function, Centre for Information Science Research (CISR), and Supercomputer Facility. The ANU's URL is `http://life.anu.edu.au`. Georgraphically closer to home, but no harder to get to via Air Mosaic, you'll find:

◆ University of North Carolina at Chapel Hill
`http://sunsite.unc.edu`

◆ Legal Information Center, Cornell Law School
`http://www.law.cornell.edu/lii.table.html`

◆ Ohio State University `http://www.cis.ohio-state.edu`

◆ Honolulu Community College `http://www.hcc.hawaii.edu`

◆ Northwestern University `http://www.acns.nwu.edu`

◆ Carnegie Mellon University `http://www.cmu.edu`

Each of these offers links to a variety of useful and remarkable documents—check 'em out.

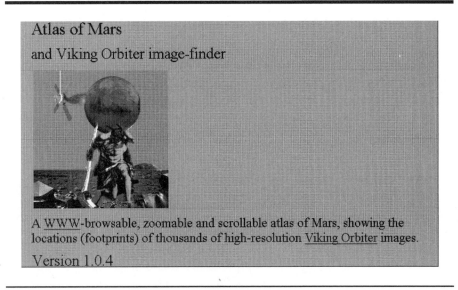

FIGURE 5.5: Care to take a gander at Mars?

 Sometimes with all the scrolling around you're doing, the display gets a bit mucked up. That is, the screen may not repaint the document window very cleanly, some words that you saw just a second ago may seem to disappear, and so on. To straighten out your screen display, select Navigate ➤ Reload from Air Mosaic's menu bar. This should do the trick.

NASA Information Services via World Wide Web

Do you want advance information about upcoming Space Shuttle missions? You can find this *and* see movies of the Dante II robot mission to the Mount Spurr volcano in Alaska, or access one of thousands of images available at the Johnson Space Center's Images server. Just go to the NASA

Information Services home page and click on <u>Hot Topics</u> for these and many more links.

What's Out There?

Space, the final frontier, is yours to explore through the NASA Information Services home page. Its URL is `http://www.nasa.gov`.

This is a terrific home page for would-be explorers. Those interested in NASA's strategy for its future (and in the future of space exploration as it proceeds into the next century) can click on <u>NASA Strategic Plan</u>. <u>Human Exploration and Development of Space</u> details the history of space exploration in terms of NASA's mission and goals. Online educational resources are also available, all through the NASA Information Services home page. Also very cool, very fresh, is the "live" map of NASA centers around the country (Figure 5.6) in the NASA Information Services home page.

What's Out There?

In the "live" map of NASA centers around the country in the NASA Information Services home page, you can click on <u>Ames Research Center</u> (`http://www.arc.nasa.gov/`) or <u>Jet Propulsion Laboratory</u> (`http://www.jpl.nasa.gov/`) in California, or <u>Johnson Space Center</u> in Houston (`http://www.jsc.nasa.gov`), or Kennedy Space Center in Florida (`http://www.ksc.nasa.gov`), to name a few. You'll jump right to the respective home page for the Web server at that location, where you can tootle around some more.

HyperDoc:
The National Library of Medicine

Here's the World-Wide-Web way to look into the National Library of Medicine, part of the U.S. National Institutes of Health in Bethesda, Maryland. The library houses over 4.5 million books, journals, reports, manuscripts, and audio-visual materials, making it the largest medical library in the world.

Of special interest to the general Net "cruiser" might be the History of Medicine exhibit (Figure 5.7) and the searchable database of nearly 60,000 images from the National Library of Medicine's History of Medicine division.

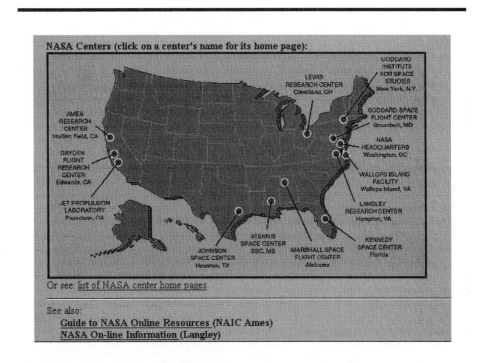

FIGURE 5.6: To find out what's up at any NASA center in the country, just click on the name of that center in this map.

What's Out There?

Everything you ever wanted to know about Western health and medicine (and perhaps even alternatives to it) can be learned from the U.S. National Library of Medicine. Its home page can be found at the URL
`http://www.nlm.nih.gov/`.

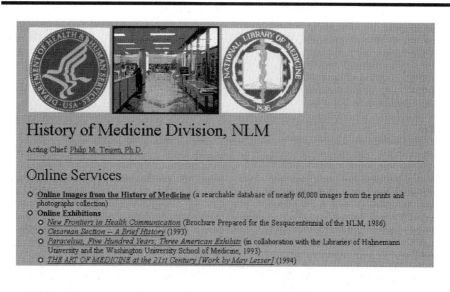

History of Medicine Division, NLM

Acting Chief: Philip M. Teigen, Ph.D.

Online Services

○ **Online Images from the History of Medicine** (a searchable database of nearly 60,000 images from the prints and photographs collection)
○ **Online Exhibitions**
   ○ *New Frontiers in Health Communication* (Brochure Prepared for the Sesquicentennial of the NLM, 1986)
   ○ *Cesarean Section -- A Brief History* (1993)
   ○ *Paracelsus: Five Hundred Years: Three American Exhibits* (in collaboration with the Libraries of Hahnemann University and the Washington University School of Medicine, 1993)
   ○ *THE ART OF MEDICINE at the 21st Century [Work by May Lesser]* (1994)

FIGURE 5.7: Be sure to stop by the History of Medicine exhibit.

To get to these from the home page, select <u>On-Line Information Services</u> (NLM, NIH, the World). Scroll to the bottom of the document and when you see the <u>History of Medicine</u> Exhibit, click on it.

Stanford University

If you want to find out what's happening at Stanford, or if you had hoped to send your kid to Stanford but know you'll never have the dough, take a look at the Stanford University home page.

What's Out There?

You can look into Stanford and what's happening there via the URL `http://www.stanford.edu/`.

This is a very broad home page with links to many a place. Big categories include:

◆ General information about Stanford University, including an overview of faculty

◆ Schools and Departments, which is a hypertext listing of the schools that make up the University, with more links to even more information

◆ Centers, which is a listing of centers associated with Stanford (like the Bechtel International Center, for example)

◆ Academic Organizations, which links you to pages for academic organizations on campus

◆ Extracurricular Organizations, which links you to pages for extracurricular organizations on campus

◆ Just Off Campus, which links you to pages for stuff off-campus that might be of interest to the campus community (the Future Fantasy bookstore, City of Palo Alto, and so on)

What's Out There?

From the Stanford home page, you can get to lots of other interesting locales, including the Hoover Institution on War, Revolution, and Peace (`http://hoover.Stanford.edu/www/welcome.html`), the Stanford Linear Accelerator Center (`http://slacvm.slac.stanford.edu/FIND/slac.html`), and the U.S-Japan Technology Management Center (`http://fuji.Stanford.edu`).

U.S. Geological Survey

The U.S. Geological Survey (USGS) boasts as one of its purposes the publishing of information about the United States' mineral land and water resources, which it has done through traditional means for many a decade. Now the USGS has a Web server.

What's Out There?

The USGS home page, providing links to resources and data related to geology, is at the URL `http://www.usgs.gov`.

You'll find links listed on the USGS home page for geologic information, minerals information, map sales, and book sales. If you live in earthquake country, you'll want to size up the seismic activity stuff—there are some nifty maps showing up-to-date earthquake information (Figure 5.8).

The USGS home page also has lots of useful information of special interest to those who work in fields related to geology. Most helpful is the directory of USGS personnel, which is an indexed, searchable database. (This feature requires forms support, which we discuss in Chapter 3.)

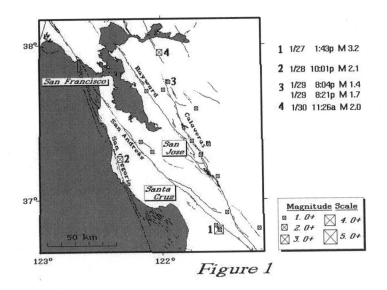

1	1/27	1:43p	M 3.2
2	1/28	10:01p	M 2.1
3	1/29	8:04p	M 1.4
	1/29	8:21p	M 1.7
4	1/30	11:26a	M 2.0

Figure 1

FIGURE 5.8: If you live in earthquake country (or if you're just curious) you'll want to check out the USGS's cool maps.

World Health Organization

Located in Switzerland, the World Health Organization is an international organization dedicated to "the attainment by all peoples of the highest possible level of health." Its home page contains hyperlinks to the World Health Organization's press releases and newsletters, including the Environmental Health Newsletter, the Global Programme on AIDS Newsletter, the Influenza Newsletter, and research newsletters on malaria and leprosy, as well as the Library Digest for Africa.

What's Out There?

The World Health Organization provides loads of information on the Web by publishing its newsletters at the URL http://www.who.ch.

Xerox PARC PubWeb

The Xerox Palo Alto Research Center (PARC) is well known as the brain trust that created such technical advances as the mouse (the one you're using as you putter on your PC), the graphical user interface, and much, much more. While you're here, be sure to check out the map viewer (Figure 5.9), which was developed by Steve Putz of PARC.

What's Out There?

Pull off the Infobahn and PARC for awhile at the URL
`http://pubweb.parc.xerox.com/;`
if you do, you can check out the way cool map viewer
(`http://pubweb.parc.com/map`).

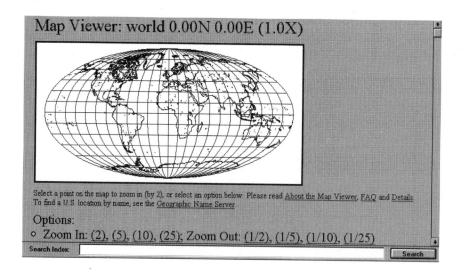

FIGURE 5.9: This map viewer is worth a pit stop.

Computer Geek Stuff

So you want to upgrade your modem? Reconfigure and upgrade your entire computer system? Find *free software*? All you need to know is where to go for all the technical and product-specific information you'll ever need. Here are some places to go—you can do your homework on the Web before you write that check to the computer store.

Cryptography, PGP, and Your Privacy

Privacy on the Net has become a major concern in the past couple of years, particularly since the U.S. Government designed the "Clipper chip," a microchip for use in digital communications devices. (Remember, Internet connections take place over *phone* lines, and as time goes on, phones are more and more often *digital* phones.) The Clipper chip is able to encrypt phone calls, making them more private than they have been, which is good news. The bad news is that the Clipper chip includes a back door that would enable "them"—U.S. intelligence and law enforcement agencies—to eavesdrop with greater ease.

Other encryption methods, such as Pretty Good Privacy (PGP), are being touted as alternatives to the government's proposed Clipper standard. (PGP is a software package that allows you to communicate securely even when you're using an insecure communications channel like e-mail or the telephone.)

The Cryptography, PGP, and Your Privacy home page (Figure 5.10) will provide you with all the background you'll need to understand these issues; it will also give you a place to get involved in grass-roots electronic activism if you care about privacy.

What's Out There?

To find out about privacy issues as they might affect you, pop in on the home page at
`http://draco.centerline.com:8080/~franl/crypto.html`.

FIGURE 5.10: About your privacy

CUI W3 Catalog

The Centre Universitaire d'Informatique (CUI for short) is a computer science research center in Geneva, Switzerland. The Centre's W3 Catalog is a searchable listing of Web resources created from several manually maintained World Wide Web lists available all over the WWW. You can enter a search string (like a list of key words) into a text box here—to indicate what you want to find information about—and the catalog will search its database, turning up whatever seems related to the key words you entered.

What's Out There?

You can access the CUI W3 Catalog (and through it, lots and *lots* of stuff on the Web) via the URL http://cuiwww.unige.ch/w3catalog.

We did a lot of the research for this chapter using the CUI W3 Catalog. Be prepared for some real serendipity to take place here. It was while we were searching for anything on women and minorities that we discovered the Little Russia and Death of Rock 'n' Roll home pages we discuss later in this chapter.

Linux: A Unix-Like Operating System for Your PC

If you're interested in fiddling around with Unix on your PC (Intel 386, 486, or Pentium), you can use Air Mosaic to gopher to a site where you can get your very own Linux software package, *for free*. Linux is a complete Unix clone that includes Emacs, X11R6, gcc, TeX/LaTeX, groff, TCP/IP, SLIP, NFS, UUCP—the works.

The Linux Documentation Project home page dishes up background information and "How To" documents about Linux and its features. Don't leave DOS without it.

What's Out There?

You'll find Linux for download at gopher://sunsite.unc.edu/11/.pub/ Linux. The Linux Documentation Project home page is at the URL http://sunsite.unc.edu/mdw/linux.html.

For more on Linux, which is a terrific operating system that's no picnic to install but a real delight to use, check out our book <u>The Complete Linux Kit</u> (Sybex, 1995). In it we talk about the ins and outs of installing and using Linux, and we even provide you with a copy of the software.

PC Week Labs

Now, even if your name isn't on the in-house routing slip, you can glean the benefits of product testing by PC Week Labs' experts. PC Week is a controlled-circulation weekly newspaper targeted at the folks who evaluate and recommend computer hardware and software for large, networked sites; PC Week Labs is a department of PC Week that conducts the testing on which reviews and technology backgrounders are based.

What's Out There?

You can get hip to PC Week Labs online through the URL `http://www.ziff.com/~pcweek/`. Check out PC Magazine, too; it's at `http://www.ziff.com/~pcmag`.

People Everywhere

Nothing says the Web has to be gender-specific, Euro-centric, or confined to the interests of the academic elite. Looking for the international Web, the alternative Web, the politicized Web? It's there, and it's growing.

The International Web

Cruise the world by Web; it's not *really* the same as going to another country, but it's faster and cheaper. The Web is global, so you can find plenty about cultures other than your own. Curious about Russia? Check out the Little Russia home page, where you can see images and documents that not only describe the culture, but give you a hyperlinked, regularly updated peek into that culture's humor through real, live translated Russian *jokes* (Figure 5.11). (You're even provided with links to explanations of the jokes, many of which make will leave you scratching your head in confusion if you don't know the cultural context.)

Australian universities are big contributors to the Web, with home pages on aboriginal studies (The Coombslists: Aboriginal and Indigenous Peoples Studies) and Asian Studies, as well as other information of interest to those who want find out about pan-Pacific cultures.

Amnesty International is an international human rights organization; it publishes a home page with information about how to contact the group and what membership involves.

What's Out There?

The Little Russia home page will clue you in to that culture; its URL is
`http://mars.uthscsa.edu/Russia/`. Find out about Aboriginal or Asian
Studies by starting at the URL
`http://coombs.anu.edu.au/CoombsHome.html`.
And to get the latest on human rights developments, turn to Amnesty International at the URL `http://cyberzine.org/html/Amnesty/ai-homepage.html`.

○ Radio Free Europe Daily Reports

○ Soviet Archives
   ○ At sunsite.unc.edu
   ○ At path.net (Includes KGB Archives)
   ○ At Texas A&M University

○ Exhibit of the Paleontological Institute of Russia

○ Russian Fonts and Software.

   Download and install the fonts before browsing Russian Network.

○ Networks

Humor. Here you can find a few Russian anecdotes translated into English. For those who are interested in Russian texts I would recommend two collections at ftp.cs.umd.edu and at sunsite.unc.edu (You will need KOI8 Russian font in order to read those anecdotes)

Links to other Russian Pages.
○ Friends and Partners - the comprehensive Information System managed by Greg Cole and Natasha Bulashova.
○ Russian and East European Network Information Center at the University of Texas at Austin. UT-REENIC provides scholars of Russia and Eastern Europe with access to academic databases and information services throughout the Internet

---

FIGURE 5.11: A sampling of Russian humor is available in Little Russia. (You'll "get" the jokes when you click on the links to explanations that place them in their correct cultural context.)

Women, Gays, and Minorities on the Web

One home page that seems at first glance to be about (just) women and computers (Women and Computing, Women and Computer Science) actually also includes information on African Americans and computing, too. It's a great starting point for the exploration of such issues as the ability of women and minorities to break into and succeed in the world of computers and computer science. Other Infobahn stops that might be of interest:

◆ The African American Culture and History home page, with sections on colonization, abolition, migration, and the WPA. (And with plans to present a major exhibition on the impact of African American culture on the American identity.)

◆ The Society and Culture: Sex home page, which provides paths to a host of lesbian, gay, and bisexual resources, ranging from pages on Domestic Partnership and Same Sex Marriage to "CyberQueer Lounge."

◆ Amnesty International's page on Lesbian and Gay Concerns.

What's Out There?

To find out more about these topics, look for the URLs
`http://www.ai.mit.edu/people/ellens/gender.html`
(Women in Computer Science),
`http://lcweb.loc,gov/exhibits/African.American/intro.html`
(African American culture),
`http://akebono.stanford.edu/yahoo/Society_and_Culture/`
`Sex/Gay_Lesbian_and_Bisexual/Resources/`
(lesbian, gay, and bisexual resources), and
`http://cyberzine.org/html/Amnesty/aihomepage.html`
(Amnesty International).

The Conservative Web

On the other side of the political coin, you can check out a home page devoted to convincing liberals of the correctness of the ultra-conservative viewpoint. The Right Side of the Web home page, featuring a photo of Ronald Reagan, is a directory of places on the Web that promote a politically conservative point of view. Topics covered include the National Review Archives and Whitewater information. There's also a link to the Newt Gingrich WWW Fan Club home page.

What's Out There?

To find out about the more conservative views expressed on the Web, go to the URL `http://www.clark.net/pub/jeffd/index.html`.

The Hip, the Cool, and the Groovy

The Web isn't just a network, it's a state of mind, a subculture, and an emerging scene. It's the electronic fast lane, where you can find out not just what's happening now, but also what's on the minds of the creative and the just plain crazy. For the truly hip and the groovy wannabes, here are some Web locales that just can't be overlooked.

Art on the Net

To get to a true art space, where artists gather, create and "hang" their work online, go to Art on the Net (a.k.a. Art.Net). Here, a variety of galleries and art styles can be seen. One piece from the online gallery is shown in Figure 5.12.

What's Out There?

To get to Art on the Net, use the URL `http://www.art.net`. To go straight to the group show gallery, use `http://www.art.net/the_gallery.html`.

FIGURE 5.12: Art on the Web

Each month, Art.Net features a visual artist, a band or musician, and a poet in its <u>Featured Artists</u> gallery. In addition, there are group shows in the Art.Net Gallery. Find out about art happenings, classes, and events around the world. (Any art-related activities can be sent to `webmaster@art.net` for posting on this server.)

CyberSight

Don't let the URL for CyberSight fool you (we thought we were going to see spaceshots of planets). CyberSight (Figure 5.13) gives you a spaceshot of the cyber*chic* planet. Here the Web is in-your-face with genuinely eccentric style.

What's Out There?

CyberSight, which is not really easy to describe other than as a doorway to what's ultra-cool and amusing on the Web, can be found using the URL `http://cybersight.com/cgi-bin/cs/s?main.gmml`.

We first found this baby while tootling around the Library of Congress home page (we talk about the Library of Congress elsewhere in this chapter). Our first visit to CyberSight included playing several rounds of interactive games (*Hangman* on the Web is charming; you can get a glimpse of it in Figure 5.14), and participating in a public opinion poll on a murder scandal that was currently grabbing a lot of media attention. This is also where we found a link to Roadkill R Us, which we describe in an upcoming section of this chapter.

Enterzone

There are lots of "literary" magazines on the Net and the Web; most of them lean more toward science fiction than real literary fare. Enterzone is a hyperzine that breaks the mold, providing a thoughtful selection of not just fiction, poetry, and essays, but also photography, paintings, and even interactive art forms (Figure 5.15). It also solicits and publishes responses to the work, adding the dimension of a salon to the basic magazine structure.

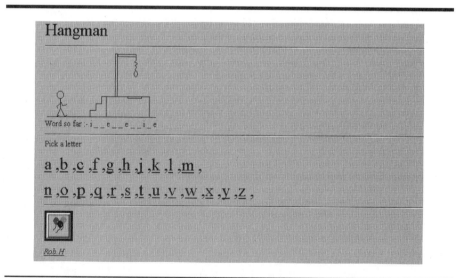

The information arcade for on-line hipsters!

Cyber Age Affirmation #6
Your Web page sucks if: Adam Curry likes it!

○ **Just a number?** Visit our O.J. Poll and be heard!

○ **Storytime... because we care.** For those traditionalists, add to our normal, everyday, linear tale entitled Bob's Mishap. For those who want full interactivity, check out our add your own adventure entitled Adventures in the Unknown. Oh, and we're not responsible for content... we do edit every so often because it can get pretty, umm, ribald.

○ **Networking.** Discuss whatever you want on our The Phlogistician's Corner, a nice little multi-dialogue interface!

○ **Blah.** Ride The Randomizer and have a piece of high culture. Or sneak through our mbox and send E-notes to us.

FIGURE 5.13: CyberSight's home page

Hangman

Word so far :- i _ _ e _ _ _ i _ e

Pick a letter

a ,b ,c ,f ,g ,h ,j ,k ,l ,m ,

n ,o ,p ,q ,r ,s ,t ,u ,v ,w ,x ,y ,z ,

Rob.H

FIGURE 5.14: Hangman is one of many interactive games on the Web.

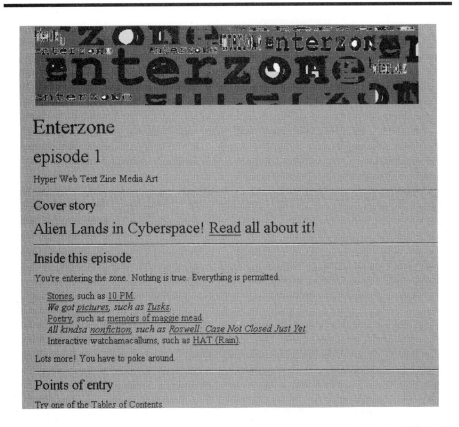

Enterzone

episode 1

Hyper Web Text Zine Media Art

Cover story

Alien Lands in Cyberspace! Read all about it!

Inside this episode

You're entering the zone. Nothing is true. Everything is permitted.

Stories, such as 10 PM.
We got pictures, such as Tusks.
Poetry, such as memoirs of maggie mead.
All kindsa nonfiction, such as Roswell: Case Not Closed Just Yet.
Interactive watchamacallums, such as HAT (Rain).

Lots more! You have to poke around.

Points of entry

Try one of the Tables of Contents.

FIGURE 5.15: Enterzone, a literary showcase

What's Out There?

Enterzone presents writing and artwork of true merit. Use the URL `http://enterzone.berkeley.edu` to find Enterzone.

Wired Magazine and HotWired

Dubbed "Wired Magazine's Rest Stop on the Infobahn," the HotWired Web server offers complete back issues of the very trendy publication, Wired. Wired was an immediate smash when it was launched in 1993.

Devoted to the cybernaut subculture, this rag is high-tech with an attitude. Its progeny, HotWired, was launched in late 1994. You can see the HotWired home page in Figure 5.16.

What's Out There?

Get HotWired via the Web server for this journal of the cybernaut subculture; the URL is `http://www.hotwired.com`.

Perhaps not surprisingly, HotWired is even cooler than its parent. Let's face it, HotWired *is* what Wired is *about*. HotWired's content in just one issue ranged from a calendar of events in Tokyo to an article about life in the South Pole.

FIGURE 5.16: HotWired is a project of Wired magazine. You can get HotWired for free via Air Mosaic on the World Wide Web.

To access HotWired, you'll have to go through the simple steps of setting up a (cost-free) account. Just follow the simple on-screen directions the first time you jump into the HotWired world; you'll have your free account in a moment or two and you won't have to go to any trouble at all next time.

Welcome to the Metaverse

This Web server (Figure 5.17) is the creation of an ex-MTV video jockey turned Internet entrepreneur; it's definitely got that Generation X edge, providing you with links to the kinds of music and weirdness this guy only talked about as a vee-jay before he got into the Web-home-page game.

What's Out There?

The Metaverse universe is right next door through the URL
`http://metaverse.com`.

The Metaverse home page is chock full o' big graphics, which move slo-o-owly across a modem connection. Accessing this home page in its entirety is going to take a while. To make the Metaverse home page show up faster, select Options ➤ Autoload Inline Images from the menu bar. This toggles off image loading, which means you won't see any pictures, but the page will be there a lot sooner.

When we took a look at Metaverse, we found a hyperlinked list of space kitsch ("collectibles and merchandise"):

◆ Starseekers Limited Edition Lithograph

◆ Skylab Space Station Fragment in Lucite Pyramid

◆ Apollo 11 25th Anniversary Video Set

◆ Apollo 11 Press Kit

FIGURE 5.17: Click in the sky portion of the image to go shopping in the metaverse.

Here's the deal: any of this stuff can be ordered via the Web! Maybe you want to order the "Space Shuttle Flight Suit, a replica of the same flight suit issued to the NASA Space Shuttle Astronauts, including patch, American flag, and NASA logo—all for $59.95 for Internet users plus $8.00 s/h and sales tax if required. The retail price is $80.00 at space centers throughout the U.S." It's yours, through the simple act of clicking the link and then providing the requested information: name, mailing address, credit card number, that sort of thing.

If you're not in a shopping frame of mind but would rather reminisce—for free—you can hyperlink your way back to the '60s via Woodstock '94. (We mentioned the Woodstock '94 home page back in Chapter 2.) Just click on an icon of two doves on a guitar handle, and (assuming you've got the sound drivers to deal with this) you'll hear some of Jimi Hendrix's most famous riffs.

You can also explore some of the facts and figures of the "real" Woodstock and see statistics describing its economic fallout.

 Keep in mind that things change on the Web at the whim of the folks who publish there. This and other home pages (and the pages they're linked to) will change to reflect the times. This is part of the Web's attraction. Don't worry, be happy: you might stumble across one truly amazing thing while you're looking for another.

That's (Sheer) Entertainment

To augment your subscriptions to entertainment rags, turn to the Web. There you'll find a variety of entertaining stuff about Tinseltown, celebrities, and products of the entertainment dream machine. As BD said, "Fasten your seatbelts, it's going to be a bumpy night," as you glide from one star-studded page to another.

Elvis Aron Presley Home Page

Die-hard Elvis fans who can't make the real trip to Memphis can take a tour of Graceland from their desktops, thanks to Andrea Berman and David Levine, creators of this Elvis home page, "created to honor Elvis and his cultural and musical legacy…." (This isn't the *only* Elvis page, incidentally. Elvis home pages crop up almost as often as Elvis sightings.)

What's Out There?

Elvis is remembered, commemorated, even revered, at the URL
`http://sunsite.unc.edu/elvis/elvishom.html`.

From this page, you can take the armchair tour through Graceland. You can also peruse an online exhibition of photos of the King, sample some Elvis tunes, and download Tiny Elvis ("this file's *h-u-g-e*") sound files for Windows. In keeping with the tour motif, there's even a guestbook to sign (Figure 5.18).

 As always, your machine must have the appropriate sound capabilities (lots o' memory along with a sound card, drivers, and maybe even speakers) to play sound files. <u>Don't try to play sound files if you don't have the stuff to do it</u>. Sound files are enormous and trying to play them without the right capabilities will crash your system.

Fill-Out Form Browser Required

Subject: I love the Elvis Pages!

Your Name: Marie Chablis

Your Email Address: mchablis@bluff.com

And I think they should have used the old Elvis on the stamp.

Any Additional Comments:

Send To: ⦿ Andrea ⦿

Press Here To Send

Return to the home page

FIGURE 5.18: Sign here to register as a visitor to the online Graceland tour.

Movie Browser Database

For the starstruck or the plain old curious, a searchable, indexed database of movie-related stuff might be just the ticket. Query it by the name of an actor or actress, the title of the film, the genre, or a quote from the movie.

From here you can also go to a hypertext listing of the Academy Award winners in many key categories, dating all the way back to 1920.

What's Out There?

You'll find a searchable database of movie information at the URL `http://www.cm.cf.ac.uk/Movies/moviequery.html` or at the URL `http://www.msstate.edu/Movies/`. A categorized list of Academy Award winners is available at `http://www.cm.cf.ac.uk:80/Movies/Oscars.html`.

World Wide Weirdness

We hardly know what to say about this. Anybody can publish a home page, and sometimes you'll run into the strangest, most wigged out stuff in the world.

Off the Beaten Web

Roadkill R Us bills itself as an Internet-based Disinformation Center and a misapplication of the World Wide Web. It seems to provide a place for folks to post pages as diverse as one on the Jihad destroying Barney and another describing a "Smut Shack."

The Death of Rock 'n' Roll presents excerpts from a book on the untimely deaths and morbid preoccupations of pop and rock personalities from Elvis to Sid Vicious and beyond. (We haven't seen Kurt Cobain there yet, but it seems inevitable.)

What's Out There?

Roadkill R Us has its spot on the Infobahn at `http://www.pencom.com/rru.html`; the Death of Rock n Roll is located at `http://alfred1.u.washington.edu:8080/~jlks/pike/DeathRR.html`.

More Practical Purposes

Not all of life is fun and games. To keep yourself informed, check out the online version of your favorite newsrag (if they publish one), or browse the Library of Congress database to single out any of millions of publications, or—if you're interested in either the broad or fine points of the Constitution—check out the doings of the U.S. Supreme Court.

The Gate

Tired of cleaning ink off your fingers after wading through the morning paper? Check out the electronic versions of the San Francisco Chronicle or Examiner. (Maybe your own town paper is on the Web, too.)

What's Out There?

The San Francisco newspapers can be found online as well as on the street. The URL for both papers is `http://cyber.sfgate.com/`. To find out about your own hometown paper you can search the CUI W3 document for *newspaper*. Maybe it'll be there, maybe it won't—new things appear on the Web daily. (We'll tell you more about searching in Chapter 6.)

Even if you don't live in S.F., you might be interested in the interactive weather map for temperatures around the U.S. and Canada published in these papers—great for planning your wardrobe before a business trip or vacation.

Library of Congress Bibliographic Service

Everybody knows about the Library of Congress, right? It's the big national repository of just about everything printed in the United States. You don't have to go to D.C. or even wait for the slow wheels of snail-mail to turn to find out what's up at the Library of Congress. You can search for whatever interests you in a few minutes of click-click-clicking.

Start at the Data Research Home Page, and then select <u>Library of Congress Basic Bibliographic Service</u>. Here you'll find a database of all the records available through the Library of Congress' Books, Maps, Music, Serials, and Visual Materials services. The database is updated weekly, and it contains millions of records. To find a specific item you can search the database by typing in a *search string* (a few words to indicate what you want to search for), as shown in Figure 5.19. Just type into the Search Index text box (it's at the bottom of the page) the author, title, ISBN or ISSN number, or the Library of Congress card number, and then press ↵. In a few seconds a screen full of data will appear, showing the results of your search (Figure 5.20).

Data Research

Welcome to the DRA copy of the LC MARC database.

This database contains the entire contents of the Library of Congress Basic Machine Readable Cataloging (MARC) Service. The *Basic Service* contains all the records contained in LC's Books All, Maps, Music, Serials, and Visual Materials services. Languages written in non-roman script appear in romanized form. As of December 1, 1993 there are 4,600,450 records in the database. This database is updated weekly.

Enter your search (including the "=")

A=
 To find authors, composers, performers, conferences, and corporate authors. Search personal names last name, first name.
 For example, **A=TWAIN, MARK**

T=
 To find a book by title or generic title. For example, **T=NUTSHELL**

S=
 To find a book by subject. For example, **S=COMPUTERS**

I=
 To find a book by ISBN. For example, **I=0120165386**

N=
 To find serial by ISSN. For example, **N=0020-9898**

L=
 To find a record by LC Card Number. For example, **L=78001165**

Search Index: `A=Frank, Thaisa`   [Search]

FIGURE 5.19: We typed the name of an author in the Search Index text box...

Frank, Thaisa

Records 1 to 3 of 3

○ Frank, Thaisa
  A brief history of camouflage / Thaisa Frank.
  Santa Rosa : Black Sparrow Press, 1992.

○ Frank, Thaisa
  Desire1 / Thaisa Frank.
  Berkeley, CA : Kelsey St. Press, c1982.

○ Frank, Thaisa
  Finding your writer's voice / Thaisa Frank and Dorothy Wall.
  New York : St. Martin's Press, 1994.

FIGURE 5.20: ...And up popped a listing of the author's books!

Supreme Court Decisions

A project of Cornell's Legal Information Institute (LII), the Supreme Court Decisions document provides a searchable database of recent Supreme Court decisions (from 1990 on) indexed by topic. You can also conduct a search based on key words. Figure 5.21 shows the bare beginning of a lengthy list that resulted from a search for matches to *irs*.

What's Out There?

A searchable database of Supreme Court decisions is available at the URL
`http://www.law.cornell.edu/supct/supct.table.html`.

NASDAQ Financial Executive Journal

This quarterly (the NASDAQ Financial Executive Journal) is a joint project of Cornell's Legal Information Institute and the NASDAQ Stock Market,

Search Result of U.S. Supreme Court Syllabi

This index was last updated Nov 9 23:01:58 1994.

Matches for **irs**:

United States v. Carlton, 114 S. Ct. 2018 (1994).

O Docket 92-1941 -- Decided June 13, 1994
O Syllabus -- OpinionConcurConcur

Newark Morning Ledger v. United States, 113 S. Ct. 1670, 118 L. Ed. 2d 288 (1993).

O Docket 91-1135 -- Decided April 20, 1993
O Syllabus -- OpinionDissent

Church of Scientology of Cal. v. United States, 113 S. Ct. 447, 121 L. Ed. 2d 313 (1992).

O Docket 91-946 -- Decided November 16, 1992
O Syllabus -- Opinion

United States v. Burke, 112 S. Ct. 1867, 119 L. Ed. 2d 34 (1992).

O Docket 91-42 -- Decided May 26, 1992
O Syllabus -- OpinionConcurConcurDissent

Search Index: irs   Search

FIGURE 5.21: If you want to look into what the U.S. Supreme Court thinks and decides, this is the place for you.

which should clue you in to what it covers. The journal provides legal and financial information to CFO-types and the investor-relations officers of NASDAQ-listed companies. This stuff might also interest other folks grappling with or interested in such issues as disclosure of preliminary merger negotiations and strategic analyses of proposed rulings by the Financial Accounting Standards Board (FASB). Does that sound like your cup of tea?

What's Out There?

To further investigate the NASDAQ Financial Executive Journal, check out the URL http://www.law.cornell.edu/nasdaq.

One Thing Leads to Another

The beauty of the World Wide Web is...well, its *webbiness*. You can start at any point on the Web and get anywhere else, anywhere in the world, because it's all interconnected. We can't tell you about everything you'll find on the Web, and we wouldn't want to. Things change. The Web changes all the time—new stuff appears there daily, and part of the wonder of Web exploration is accidentally coming across the unexpected, the unusual, or even the outrageous as you tinker about.

After looking through these last two chapters, you should have some ideas about where to get started and about the range of stuff that's available. Cruising the Web is your game now—have a grand old time.

Now you probably want to know how to find just what you're looking for without cruising. In the next chapter, we'll look into some great tools for searching and finding whatever you're looking for on the Web.

Tools and Techniques for Searching and Finding

Okay, so everyone knows the World Wide Web is growing at a mind-boggling rate. Then how does the intrepid Web cruiser find what he or she is looking for among all of what's out there? How does anyone know even where to *begin* a search? As you use the Internet—especially the Web—you may find yourself sucked into a black hole of pointing-and-clicking, following hyperlinks with complete abandon and fascination, yet coming up with little information that's relevant to the project at hand. (That's why they call it *cyberspace*....)

Let's step back for a second and take a look at gathering information in ways that aren't so willy-nilly. The Web is a bona fide research tool, after all—let's find out how it can be used to find information on focused topics. Say, for example, you work in the planning department of a large corporation and you need to write a business report about the current cause célèbre of corporate America—"reengineering."

Say you want to pepper your report with statistical data—productivity levels in American business over the past ten years, unemployment levels, inflation rates, and so on. You also want to describe the viewpoints of financial, economic, and business experts, and to address forecasts for the future of business.

The Web is gigantic, webby, and *growing*. (We've said this before.) You just can't expect everything on the Web to be contained in any one place or searchable through any one tool. To do your Web research, whether it is on our example topic or any other topic, you'll use a number of tools:

◆ The archive of past NCSA What's New pages

◆ The World Wide Web Worm

◆ Veronica, the complete gopher index

In the rest of this chapter, we'll describe each of these tools, what it's good for, and when its use is appropriate.

The NCSA What's New Page Archives

We've talked earlier in this book about the NCSA What's New document—it lists new services on the Web and it's updated monthly, so it's a great starting place for your Web travels. Now what do you suppose happens when the NCSA What's New document is updated? All those handy announcements don't just go away, they're moved (by the Internet's invisible helpers) from the current What's New document into a database. Here's the big news: You can use Air Mosaic to search this archival database.

The archive of What's New pages is kept in a comprehensive database by the people at the Centre Universitaire d'Informatique, at the University of Geneva in Switzerland. Here you'll find not only the announcements from the NCSA What's New pages, but also items of interest they've gathered from other Web indexes. Searching this database will give you quick entrée to a wide variety of topics and sources of information.

 To access and search the NCSA What's New document, you'll use the CUI W3 Catalog page as a tool.

What's Out There?

You can access the searchable archive of What's New pages with the URL `http://cuiwww.unige.ch/w3catalog`.

About Searching the NCSA What's New Archive

Searching NCSA What's New page archive is a snap. To search the archive, you'll use the CUI W3 Catalog. In a nutshell, all you have to do is open the CUI W3 Catalog, type in some text that describes what interests you, click a button, and sit back and watch a page of links appear on your screen. Let's take a closer look.

Opening the Page

To search the What's New page archive, you must first open the CUI W3 Catalog:

1. Select File ➤ Open URL from the menu bar. The Open URL dialog box will appear.
2. In the Open URL dialog box's text box, type **http://cuiwww.unige.ch/w3catalog**.
3. Click on the OK button. The dialog box will disappear, the "world" will be animated, and in a few seconds the CUI W3 Catalog page will appear (Figure 6.1).

Performing the Search

With the CUI W3 Catalog page on screen, now is the time to start searching.

1. A text box will be visible near the top of the page. Type a word or two that describes what interests you into the text box. (For example, to find information about baseball, type **baseball** into the text box.)

FIGURE 6.1: The CUI W3 page is your path to old (but still valuable) NCSA What's New pages.

2. Click on the Submit button. This will send the text you typed to the database, where a search will be performed like magic. If the topic of interest is part of any entry in the database, a page containing information (or at least a mention) of that topic will appear. (Figure 6.2 shows what we found when we searched for *baseball*.)

> The CUI W3 Catalog searches many Web resources, not just the NCSA What's New page archives. When you do a search, don't be surprised if you get a page that includes items from other sources in addition to NCSA What's New pages.

In the pages you see as a result of your search, you'll find the now familiar underlined (and often blue) text that represents links to other pages. These links behave just like the links in any document—click on a link to go directly to the item it describes.

Performing More Complicated Searches with CUI W3

You aren't limited to searching for simple words like *baseball* or *linux* in the NCSA What's New page archives. You can type far more complex *strings* (lists) into the text box to make your search more specific. This is

W3 Catalog

Please enter a search word/pattern or provide a Perl regular expression:

[Submit] [_____]

NB: Searches are case-insensitive.

Result of search for "baseball":

August 15, 1994: The World Wide Web of Sports, available from the Telemedia, Networks and Systems group at MIT's Laboratory for Computer Science, now features daily highlights from World Cup Soccer. The World Wide Web of Sports page provides a customization feature where users can choose which links appear on their personalized sports page. The sports pages also feature daily highlights from Major League Baseball and links to other sports pages around the Web. In other news, the TNS group announces the development of the MapMaker program, a Mosaic-integrated assistant for building imagemaps on any image. Also be sure to check out their Cool Video Demos. (nwn)

October 25, 1994
○ :Sell-it on the WWW provides advertising on the WWW. There are nearly 20 companies right now whose products range from baseball cards to computer hardware & software to gourmet coffee to publications to computer consulting. Check out all these great features plus much more at Sell-it on the WWW. Great for gifts! Also, if you'd like to advertise on the server for $10 a month, please see the server or e-mail dknight@powergrid.electriciti.com. (nwn)

August 15, 1994: The World Wide Web of Sports, available from the Telemedia, Networks and Systems group at MIT's Laboratory for Computer Science, now features daily highlights from World Cup Soccer. The World Wide Web of Sports

FIGURE 6.2: Searching for baseball came up with these entries, each of which has links to the actual pages.

no simple matter, however; it involves entering a combination of text and special symbols, along with having some knowledge of discrete mathematics. The techniques of performing a complex search are beyond the scope of this book, but you can find a how-to discussion on this topic by clicking on the Perl regular expression link on the CUI W3 Catalog page.

The World Wide Web Worm

The NCSA What's New page archive is a great place to find some terrifically useful pages on the Web, it lists only those pages that have been submitted to NCSA for inclusion in the What's New page's announcements. Plenty of wonderful Web pages are never listed on the What's New page.

To broaden your search beyond what's known to the What's New folks, use the World Wide Web Worm (the *Worm*). The heart of the Worm is a program that burrows through the Web, searching thousands of home pages for links to other pages, then compiling both the URL and title of

each of these pages into one gigantic searchable database. At the time of this writing, the Word Wide Web Worm database includes references to some 300,000 objects on the Web; it is accessed well over 2 million times per month.

Opening the World Wide Web Worm Page

To search the World Wide Web Worm database, you must open the World Wide Web Worm page. Here you'll find an on-screen form into which you'll type the *search criteria* (what you want to search for). Then you'll "submit" the search to the database. When the search is complete, a page will appear with links to other pages that match your search criteria.

The first step in using the World Wide Web Worm is to open its page in Air Mosaic.

1. Select File ➤ Open URL from the menu bar. The Open URL dialog box will appear.

2. In the Open URL dialog box's text box, type the URL for the World Wide Web Worm page

http://www.cs.colorado.edu/home/mcbryan/WWWW.html

3. Click on the OK button. The dialog box will disappear, the "world" will be animated, and in a few seconds the World Wide Web Worm page will appear (Figure 6.3).

What's Out There?

The World Wide Web Worm can be surfaced with the URL
`http://www.cs.colorado.edu/home/mcbryan/WWWW.html`.

> # WWWW - the WORLD WIDE WEB WORM
>
> Best of the Web '94 - Best Navigational Aid. Oliver McBryan
>
> The Worm scours the Web for resources and provides search capabilities on its database of 300,000 multimedia objects. Run: Sept 5. **Usage: 330,000 per month.**
>
> ○ Introduction and Definitions
> ○ Search and Search Examples
> ○ Known Bugs - CERN Proxy Server
> ○ Register a New Resource
> ○ Published paper on WWWW.
>
> Select:
> 1. Search only in Titles of citing documents
> 2. Search only in Names of citing documents
> 3. Search all Citation Hypertext
> 4. Search all Names of Cited URL's
>
> Keywords: [   ] [Start Search]
>
> ## Definitions

FIGURE 6.3: The World Wide Web Worm is a powerful search utility that searches the Web and catalogs the URL and title of every page that it finds, making a database of that information available to you.

Searching the World Wide Web Worm Database

With the World Wide Web page open, you are ready to start digging up dirt—er, *data*. Take a look at the page; it includes text that tells you about the Worm and even some example searches. It also includes links to yet more information about the Worm.

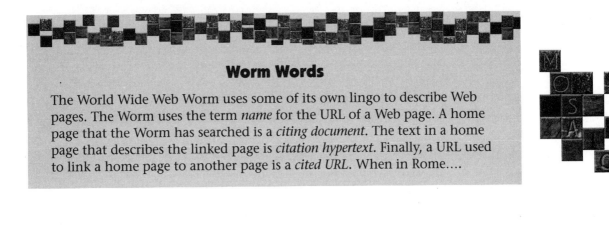

Worm Words

The World Wide Web Worm uses some of its own lingo to describe Web pages. The Worm uses the term *name* for the URL of a Web page. A home page that the Worm has searched is a *citing document*. The text in a home page that describes the linked page is *citation hypertext*. Finally, a URL used to link a home page to another page is a *cited URL*. When in Rome....

A lot of pages are known to the Worm, but not every page is. Only those that are on a home page the Worm knows about or those that are referenced by a home page will be in the Worm's database. That's why you may not find something now that you think you've seen before. A hypertext reference or page that isn't a home page or doesn't appear anywhere on another home page won't be in the list.

To perform a search using the Worm:

1. In the World Wide Web Worm page, the box labeled *Select* controls the way the Worm's database will be searched for documents. The options are:

Search only in Titles of citing documents Searches the titles of all the home pages in the Worm's database.

Search only in Names of citing documents Searches the URLs of all the home pages in the Worm's database.

Search all Citation Hypertext Searches the hypertext (the text that represents links to other pages) in the home pages in the Worm's database.

Search all Names of Cited URLs Searches those URLs in the home pages that are linked to other pages.

To select an option, click on its name. (The selected option will always be highlighted.)

You'll have the best luck if you select either *Search only in Titles of citing documents* or *Search all Citation Hypertext*. Either of these searches the English text that describes a page, not the URL for that page. (What you'll get back is a list of documents that contain the text you specified in either their titles or their descriptions.) If you know part of the URL you're looking for, select *Search only in Names of citing documents* or *Search all Names of Cited URLs*. Either of these options (see Figure 6.4) searches the URLs for specific documents. (What you'll get back this time is a list of documents that match the URL you specified in part.)

```
           1. Search only in Titles of citing documents
Select:    2. Search only in Names of citing documents
           3. Search all Citation Hypertext
           4. Search all Names of Cited URL's

Keywords: finance|                                        Start Search
```

FIGURE 6.4: The Worm is going to search its database for <u>finance</u>.

2. Now that you've told the Worm how it should search, you'll tell the Worm what it seeks. In the *Keywords* box, type some text to point the Worm on its way.

 The developer of the Worm, Oliver McBryan, recommends keeping your searches to a single word rather than a string of text so they will go faster.

3. Click on the Start Search button to begin the search. In a few seconds a new page will appear listing everything it found in the database that matched what you told the Worm to find. (Figure 6.5 shows the result of a search for *finance*.)

finance

Return to Searching

1. Business, Finance, Economics
   ○ cited in: http://www.pitt.edu/~cjp/rees.html

2. Business, management, accounting, banking, finance
   ○ cited in: http://www.demon.co.uk/bookshop/mail.html

3. Commissariat on Finances
   ○ cited in: http://sunsite.unc.edu/expo/soviet.exhibit/r2commss.html

4. Commissariat on Finances
   ○ cited in: http://sunsite.unc.edu/expo/soviet.exhibit/r2commss.html

5. Commissariat on Finances
   ○ cited in: http://sunsite.unc.edu/expo/soviet.exhibit/overview.html

6. Committee on Finance
   ○ cited in: http://www.city.palo-alto.ca.us/pa-city/people/city-government/directory-by-org.html

7. Committee on Finance
   ○ cited in: http://www.city.palo-alto.ca.us/people/city-government/directory-by-org.html

8. Committee on Finance
   ○ cited in: http://www.city.palo-alto.ca.us/pa-city/people/city-government/directory-by-org.html

FIGURE 6.5: This list of financial things on the Web is the result of our search for <u>finance</u>.

Sometimes your search of the Worm will turn up a page saying that nothing was found. This happens not just when nothing matched your search criteria, but sometimes when the Worm is overcrowded. (The folks who maintain the Worm are working on this problem.) If a search that you believe should have worked comes up with nothing, try the search again later.

Performing More Complicated Searches with the Worm

You don't have to limit yourself to entering simple text as search criteria in the Keywords box. To conduct more complex searches, you can use a number of special characters. The Worm page itself contains information on using these techniques to make your searches more powerful and specific. Here are a couple of examples:

What You Can Type	What It Means
Apple.*Mac	Anything with *Apple* followed by *Mac* (like *Apple PowerMac* or *Apple Macintosh*)
(Microsoft | Novell) DOS	Anything that includes *Microsoft DOS* or *Novell DOS*

Usually you won't have to resort to these kinds of complex search criteria; searching the Worm using simple text is often the best way to go.

Veronica

Veronica is a self-updating database of gopher documents. Gopher documents, as you'll recall from previous discussion, are usually text files (but sometimes telnet links to other computers, searchable databases, or graphics files). *Veronica* is an acronym that stands for Very Easy Rodent-Oriented Net-wide Index to Computerized Archives. (The rodent reference is, of course, *gopher*.) Often you'll hear old-timers (essentially people who've used the Net for more than a year) say something like "You can gopher to Veronica to find that."

Air Mosaic can access gopher servers, making the use of Veronica a breeze, but you'll find the NCSA What's New archive and the World Wide Web Worm to be far more useful Web-searching tools.

Like the World Wide Web Worm, Veronica locates things on the Web by searching through words in titles, rather than by doing a full-fledged search of the document. For purposes of a Veronica search, the *title* is the name of the resource as listed on its home gopher server. Veronica "knows" about an incredible 10 million documents stored on 4,500 different gopher servers!

You can access Veronica from any of scads of gopher servers (remember, you can access any menu on a gopher server just like it was any other "page" on the Web) but we're going to concentrate here on just one page— the one kept on the University of Minnesota gopher server—as an example.

Gopher History in a Nutshell

The University of Minnesota gopher server is the mother of 'em all; that's because the University of Minnesota *invented* gopher. Gopher had its origins in an idea similar to the one that inspired HTML—the gopher's inventors wanted a way to organize information. The solution they came up with was to use menus from which you could pick items that led to documents—it's the same concept as hyperlink, but without the nice graphics and "lightning fast" linking HTML offers by actually placing the links in the documents.

As Mosaic and the use of HTML become more common, you might think gopher would fade away. But gopher is a mature and workable system that's being incorporated into the Web. You can use gopher with Air Mosaic as another one of your Net cruising tools.

Opening Up a Veronica Page

To use Veronica, you must open up a page in Air Mosaic that includes links to Veronica. Here we are using a page from the University of Minnesota's gopher server to get to Veronica. As you cruise around other gopher servers using Air Mosaic, you'll probably find other places to gain entry into Veronica.

To open up a page in Air Mosaic with links to Veronica:

1. Select File ➤ Open URL from the menu bar. The Open URL dialog box will appear.
2. In the Open URL dialog box's text box, type the URL

   gopher://gopher.tc.umn.edu:70/11/Other%20Gopher %20and%20Information%20Servers/Veronica

Okay, so this URL is long. Remember, gopher was originally designed as a menu system. The URL shown has as its task opening layers of menu choices. To make opening Veronica faster in the future, add this URL to your Hotlist.

3. Click on the OK button. The dialog box will disappear, the "world" will be animated, and in a few seconds a gopher page like the one shown in Figure 6.6 will appear.

What's Out There?

You can call on Veronica using the URL
`gopher://gopher.tc.umn.edu/11/Other%20Gopher %20and%20Information%20Servers/Veronica.`

Searching Veronica

Great. We'll start searching in a minute. But first, take a look at the Veronica page and notice that from this page you can search Veronicas located at

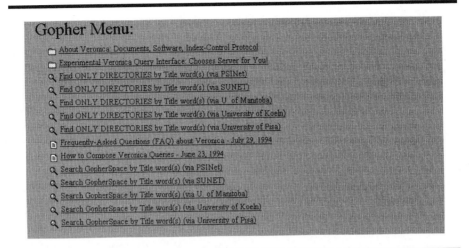

Gopher Menu:
- 📁 About Veronica: Documents, Software, Index-Control Protocol
- 📁 Experimental Veronica Query Interface: Chooses Server for You!
- 🔍 Find ONLY DIRECTORIES by Title word(s) (via PSINet)
- 🔍 Find ONLY DIRECTORIES by Title word(s) (via SUNET)
- 🔍 Find ONLY DIRECTORIES by Title word(s) (via U. of Manitoba)
- 🔍 Find ONLY DIRECTORIES by Title word(s) (via University of Koeln)
- 🔍 Find ONLY DIRECTORIES by Title word(s) (via University of Pisa)
- 📄 Frequently-Asked Questions (FAQ) about Veronica - July 29, 1994
- 📄 How to Compose Veronica Queries - June 23, 1994
- 🔍 Search GopherSpace by Title word(s) (via PSINet)
- 🔍 Search GopherSpace by Title word(s) (via SUNET)
- 🔍 Search GopherSpace by Title word(s) (via U. of Manitoba)
- 🔍 Search GopherSpace by Title word(s) (via University of Koeln)
- 🔍 Search GopherSpace by Title word(s) (via University of Pisa)

FIGURE 6.6:   Here is the University of Minnesota's gopher menu, which includes access to Veronica.

many different places (such as PSINet in the USA, University of Manitoba in Canada, and the University of Pisa in Italy). All these Veronicas should provide essentially the same information, but they're all maintained by different people at different times, so the information might not be completely in sync from one Veronica to another. Also, one server may be busier at any given time than another, so response time may vary from server to server.

A big trick to using Veronica is to select a Veronica based on its proximity to you while taking into account whether that Veronica shows fast response speeds right now. (The only way for you to know about the response speeds is to use Veronica enough to get a feel for which places are faster and when.)

A search of gopherspace (all gopher servers throughout the Internet) by keywords in titles will turn up all types of resources—text documents, image files, binary files, gopher directories, and so on—whose names contain the specified search word or words. On the other hand, a search of gopher directories by keywords contained in titles only looks at gopher directories, not documents. That provides fewer places from which to choose but places that may be more focused.

To start you search of Veronica:

1. With your gopher page open, click on one of the following links to Veronica:

Click On	To Search For
Search GopherSpace by Title word(s) (via PSINet)	Gopher documents by using the Veronica server at Performance Systems, Inc. in New York State.
Find ONLY DIRECTORIES by title word(s) (via PSINet)	Directories containing gopher documents by using the Veronica server at Performance Systems, Inc. in New York State.
Search GopherSpace by Title word(s) (via SUNET)	Gopher documents by using the Veronica server at Swedish University Network in Sweden.
Find ONLY DIRECTORIES by title word(s) (via SUNET)	Directories of gopher documents by using the Veronica server at Swedish University Network in Sweden.
Search GopherSpace by Title word(s) (via U. of Manitoba)	Gopher documents by using the Veronica server at the University of Manitoba in Canada.
Find ONLY DIRECTORIES by title word(s) (via U. Of Manitoba)	Directories of gopher documents by using the Veronica server at the University of Manitoba in Canada.
Search GopherSpace by Title word(s) (via University of Koeln)	Gopher documents by using the Veronica server at the University of Koeln in Germany.

Click On	**To Search For**
<u>Find ONLY DIRECTORIES by title word(s) (via University of Koeln)</u>	Directories of gopher documents by using the Veronica server at the University of Koeln in Germany.
<u>Search GopherSpace by Title word(s) (via University of Pisa)</u>	Gopher documents by using the Veronica server at the University of Pisa in Italy.
<u>Find ONLY DIRECTORIES by title word(s) (via University of Pisa)</u>	Directories of gopher documents by using the Veronica server at the University of Pisa in Italy.

A page will appear that lets you then search the selected Veronica database. Figure 6.7 shows what happened when we selected <u>Search GopherSpace by Title word(s) (via PSINet)</u>.

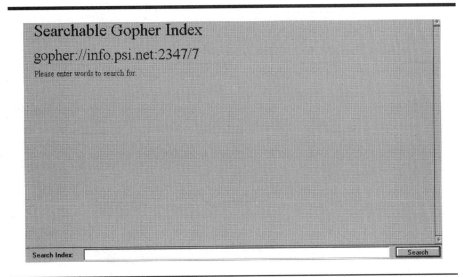

FIGURE 6.7: Type whatever you're looking for into the Search Index text box.

2. In the Search Index text box at the bottom of the page, enter the text for your search. For example, to search for information about photography, type either **photo** or **photography**.

Don't worry about using upper- and lowercase letters; Veronica searches ignore capitalization.

3. Click on the Search button. The world will become animated and in a few seconds a page will appear listing documents that contain text matching what you typed in as search criteria (see Figure 6.8).

When you construct your search, keep in mind that if you use multiple words as your search criteria (like women in photography) only items that contain all of the words you indicated will be considered matches. This may keep you from finding everything out there that's related to your topic, or it may help you to find only what you need. At the same time, think about the type of information you're looking for and into what broader categories it might be filed, then tailor your search to your needs. For example, a specific topic such as Honda might be found by searching for the more general automobile.

With your page of items matching your search criteria in view, you can click on links to cruise around just as you would with any other page.

Performing More Complicated Searches with Veronica

Veronica lets you control aspects of the search by adding what it calls "flags" to your search string.

Gopher Menu:

- rec-photo-faq
- rec-photo
- photo.exe
- Photo Request
- photo
- photo
- Digitized photo negatives
- Re: Digitized photo negatives
- Philip Fried Digitized photo negs.
- RE: Philip Fried Digitized photo negs.
- Photo CD
- Re: Photo CD
- Re: Photo CD
- Re: Photo CD
- 1.50 beta & Photo-CD plug-i
- Re: 1.50 beta & Photo-CD plug-i
- President in Photo Op with Belgian PM Klaes, Brussels, 1994-1-9

FIGURE 6.8: We searched gopherspace for the word "photo" and came up with this list of items.

Using Flags to Search for Files

Flags are made up of dashes followed by letters and numbers. They can control things like the type of file you want to search for (for example, text files or GIF graphics files) or the number of items to find. The Veronica screen itself provides links to more information about the use of flags. Here are a couple of examples of useful flags.

Maximum Number of Documents You can use the m (for maximum) flag to control the maximum number of documents returned from a search. Without using the flag, Veronica will return up to the first 200 documents that match the search criteria. By adding the m flag, you can either increase or decrease this number. To use the m flag, add −mn (where n is the number of matches to return) to the end of your search criteria.

Type of Document The Type of Document flag, t, controls what type of document you wish to find. To use it, add −tn to the end of the search string; n is a number or letter that specifies the type of document you

want to find. The following table summarizes the more common documents you can search for:

Replace <u>n</u> With	To Find
0	Text file
1	Directory
4	Mac HQX file
5	PC binary file
7	Gopher menu
8	Telnet session
9	Binary file
s	Sound file
i	Non-GIF image file
M	MIME multipart/mixed message
g	GIF image
h	HTML file

Using -m at the end of your search criteria without a number or letter following it will find all the objects that match the other search criteria—in other words, if you don't enter a number like those shown above with the -m, you might as well not use -m at all.

Using Operators to Refine or Broaden a Search

If you enter as your search criteria a simple multiple word search like *American business*, Veronica will search for instances of both words together, *American* and *business*, in either order. The search will, for example, find objects categorized as *business, American*. Veronica interprets the entry *American business* as *American* AND *business*, where AND is a "logical operator" being used to establish a relationship between the two words for the search.

You can also use the operators NOT (to indicate to Veronica that you want *business* NOT *American*, for example) and OR (to indicate to Veronica that you want *business* OR *leisure* or some such thing). You can even make things more complex by using opening and closing parentheses. As an example of this,

```
((business OR leisure) travel) NOT American
```

will find anything pertaining to *business or leisure travel*, excluding *American business or leisure travel*.

Search strings are interpreted from right to left, and operators are interpreted as they are encountered.

It's probably best to avoid using OR alone because of the wide range and volume of stuff that search might produce. Instead, use OR in conjunction with parentheses to tightly focus your search.

Now You Know

Having read this far, you now know everything you need to know to check out what's on the Web. Maybe at this point you'd like to find out how to publish your own Web pages, including how to make your own home page. In the next chapter we'll look at HTML and how to use it.

Part Three:

Beyond the Basics

You Too Can Be a Web Publisher

By now, having used Air Mosaic to roam the World Wide Web, you've seen the power of hypertext firsthand. You've seen that hypertext acts as both the Web's glue and its strands—binding it together yet hiding the complexities of Internet cruising. HTML (the HyperText Markup Language) is the *standard* (the agreed-upon system of marking up text to create pages and links) that makes the Web possible. What started out as an experiment has been embraced by the Internet as *the* means of providing information. It will probably come as no surprise that HTML, in the spirit of the Internet, is published and readily available. *Anyone* can use this standard to publish hypertext documents.

Maybe now you want to get into the act. This chapter will tell you how to get started as a Web publisher. There are five basic steps to creating a Web page:

- ◆ Organizing your concepts and materials
- ◆ *Storyboarding* (sketching out) the page(s) you intend to create
- ◆ Building a prototype
- ◆ Testing the prototype and making adjustments
- ◆ Putting your page on a server

This stuff isn't impossibly difficult—it helps to have a little experience, but *hey,* everybody's got to start somewhere. Let's look at how HTML works and how you, too, can write HTML documents.

To actually publish a document for public viewing on the Web, you'll need access to an <u>http-</u> or <u>ftp</u> <u>server</u>. Don't expect to run this server on your PC with a dial-up connection to the Internet. Many Internet service providers provide access to an http- or ftp server at no additional cost. (We'll go over this in more detail at the end of this chapter.)

What's Out There?

You'll find a highly insightful style guide devoted to the use of HTML at `http://www.w3.org/hypertext/WWW/Provider/Style/Overview.html`.

About HTML:
The HyperText Markup
Language

There is plenty to know about HTML and creating and publishing Web documents. Sadly, we'll have to leave the finer points to the bigger books, but let's go over the basics: how to make the heads in your documents appear in big, bold letters; how to link your documents to other documents; and how to embed pictures in your document.

The documents you see on the World Wide Web via Air Mosaic look nice, but there's a bit of minor technological magic going on. In actuality, the files for these documents are stored on some machines as plain ASCII text files—unlike word processing files, these ASCII text files include no formatting, and they employ no fancy fonts or attributes like bold or italics. They are plain as plain can be. (See Figure 7.1.) All the special effects that

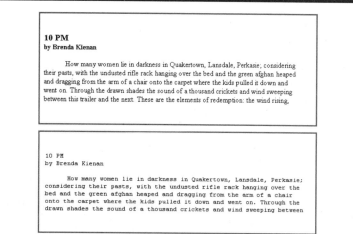

FIGURE 7.1: The document shown on the top was created in a word processing program; shown on the bottom is the same document in ASCII text format. Notice that the font and all the attributes (bold and italic) are lost in the transition.

What's Out There?

You'll find loads of resources for creating Web pages at the WWW & HTML Developer's JumpStation—the URL is `http://oneworld. wa.com/htmldev/devpage/dev-page.html`.

you see in a Web document—bold, italic, links to other documents—are represented in the ASCII text files with special codes that also are made up of plain text characters.

This means, luckily, that you can use any word processor (Word, Word-Perfect, Ami Pro, whatever) or text editor (DOS Edit) to create your HTML documents. We use Microsoft Word for Windows to create our HTML documents, but you can use any word processor or text editor you like. The only inflexible condition here is that you must save the file as plain

ASCII text before Air Mosaic—or any other Web browser—can display it. So make sure your word processor can do that (most can).

Okay, so we just made the big point that you don't need a special HTML editor, yet there are HTML editors available. Though unnecessary for writing basic HTML documents, an HTML editor certainly would prove beneficial when you're dealing with hundreds of pages of text. A good HTML editor can help you enter HTML commands and verify that you have all the details correct, making it easier to ensure that your Web documents will be displayed correctly in a Web browser.

What's Out There?

A number of freely available programs and add-ins to word processors exist to help you write HTML documents. These can be of great use when you are writing longer documents or complex Web pages. CU_HTML, a template that works with Word for Windows (versions 2 and 6) and was developed at the Chinese University of Hong Kong, is available at the URL `http://www.cuhk.hk/csc/cu_html/cu_html.html`. HotMetal for Windows from SoftQuad (a favorite) is available at `http://www.sq.com/hm-ftp.htm`, and html-helper-mode for EMACS is available at the URL `http://www.santafe.edu/~nelson/tools`.

The Elements of Web Page Design

Your Web home page will be accessed by anywhere from dozens to hundreds-of-thousands of people per day. You'll want it to convey clearly and concisely the message you intend to promote (whether that's your resume, an account of what's happening at the local soda pop machine, or your company's policy on hiring technical professionals). In this section, we'll cover some basic guidelines for successful Web page design, tossing out for your consideration all the big-hitting tips we've picked up in our Internet travels.

Just What Is a Markup Language?

Traditionally, a markup language uses defined sequences of control characters or commands embedded within a document. These commands control what the document looks like when it is output to, say, a printer. When you print the document, the control character sequences or commands format the document, displaying such elements as bold headlines, subheads, bulleted items, and the like. IBM's Document Control Language (DCL) and Microsoft's Rich Text Format (RTF) are two examples of markup languages used by many word processing programs to create the effects you see on screen and in print like bold headlines, subheads, bulleted items, and the like.

HTML differs from other markup languages, however, in its overall approach. HTML is unlike typical markup languages in that it is not so much concerned with typefaces and character attributes, but rather the internal document makeup itself. In a language like DCL, you would use commands to indicate the typeface, font size, and style of the text *in a document*. In HTML, the commands indicate the headings, normal paragraphs, lists, and even links *to other Web pages*.

HTML is derived from the Standard Generalized Markup Language (SGML), which has come into increasingly common usage in word processing and other programs for creating print documents. HTML follows the SGML paradigm in that it uses *tags* to do its formatting. Tags are pieces of coding that usually, but not always, come in pairs of start-tag and end-tag, marking off *elements*.

When you create HTML documents, bear in mind that the HTML "standard" is in a state of development, with changes happening to accommodate changes in the World Wide Web and its attending software. If you try something that works one day and not the next, it may be that the standard has changed.

Another minor annoyance is that not all Web browsers support all HTML extensions, or they may support other aspects of the HTML language differently. Be this as it may, the basic HTML structure that is presented in this chapter should work well in most instances.

Get Organized

The best way to get started in the design of your home page is to organize your assets: the existing documents and images you want to work with, for example. Think about the message you want to convey and what types of images or text might be appropriate (is it fun and lighthearted or seriously corporate?).

What's Out There?

You'll want to find out everything you can about copyright issues; this will come up both when you want to protect your own material and when you want to use something you've "found" on the Net. (That's not always legal.) A U.S. copyright law page published by Cornell University is at the URL `http://www.law.cornell.edu/topics/copyright.html` and a FAQ (frequently asked question) list published by Ohio State is at the URL `http://www.cis.ohio-state.edu/hypertext/faq/usenet/Copyright-FAQ/top.html`.

Create a Storyboard

With the stuff you want to work with in hand, sit down with paper and pencil (or some nifty drawing software) and plot the thing out. *Storyboard* (sketch) your home page and each page it will link to; include all the elements you're considering (text, images, buttons, hot links), and don't be afraid to make adjustments. If your original concept doesn't flow nicely, can it and start again. *You can't do too much advance planning*.

Build a Prototype and Test It

When you've got your pages planned, go ahead and build a prototype. Then test it, test it, and *test it again*. Ask friends and colleagues to try it out and comment, and do all the fine tuning you can. You want to make public your best work, not some funky work-in-progress.

18 Top Tips for Winning Page Design

You have two seconds to grab your reader's attention. That's common knowledge in advertising and publishing circles. You can't go wrong if you follow these basic tips for designing an attention-getting, successful home page:

◆ Before you start, organize your concepts and materials; sketch out your ideas and how they'll work.

◆ Make the title precise, catchy, and descriptive.

◆ Keep the page active but loose; don't let it get crowded with images, text, or "doo-dads."

◆ Put the important items at the top of the page; don't assume anyone will ever scroll down.

◆ Balance white space; balance large and small images and blocks of text.

◆ Avoid using too many fonts.

◆ Anything that looks like a button should behave like a button.

◆ Avoid links that go nowhere, and don't create two links with different names that go to the same place.

◆ Make your links on descriptive and accurate words or images. Avoid the generic; don't link on the word "here."

◆ Use images that contain less than 50 colors.

◆ Include thumbnails of larger, downloadable images.

◆ Remember that people will access your page using different browsers (various types of Mosaic, Cello, Netscape, etc.) and different platforms (Windows, Unix, Mac).

◆ Keep filenames short; make them consistent.

(continued on next page)

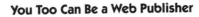

(continued from previous page)

◆ Tell people the size of downloadable files if you include them.

◆ Find out if you need permission to use text or images created by someone else.

◆ Establish who's going to be Webmaster and make a link on your page leading to the Webmaster.

◆ Build a prototype and test it thoroughly. Do the fine tuning before you announce your page.

◆ Announce and publicize your page wherever possible.

You can test your prototype without making it public. At the end of this chapter you'll find a section titled Using Air Mosaic to Check Your HTML Document that tells you how.

A Quick Look at Successful Web Page Designs

The best way to get ideas and to explore creating a winning Web page is to study examples. We've been showing you Web pages throughout this book; here we're going to take a look at a few especially well-designed pages, pointing out what makes them so terrific.

Some of the Web pages we show here are a bit out of an amateur Webspinner's range—we're including them anyway, to give you an idea of the possibilities.

A Sleek, Space Age Wonder

NASA has developed an understandably strong Web presence. Here's a sleek page (Figure 7.2) that uses a large, striking graphic with links to other pages (in the form of thumbnails) embedded in it. While the graphic in this page is large and takes a while to load, the result is pretty eye-catching and very easy to use. This home page provides access to a wealth of information about NASA.

What's Out There?

The NASA universe is yours to explore at the URL htpp://www.nasa.gov.

An Understandable Book Metaphor

While the graphics aren't slick, Novell used a very apt book metaphor (Figure 7.3) as the entryway into its Web offerings; users can click on the "title" of any "book" for information on the topic of interest.

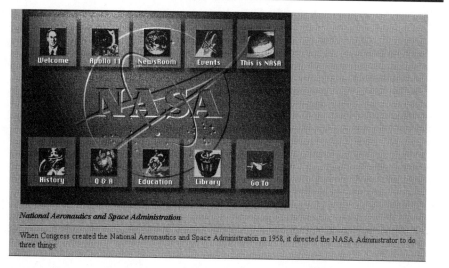

FIGURE 7.2: The NASA Public Affairs home page is a real beauty.

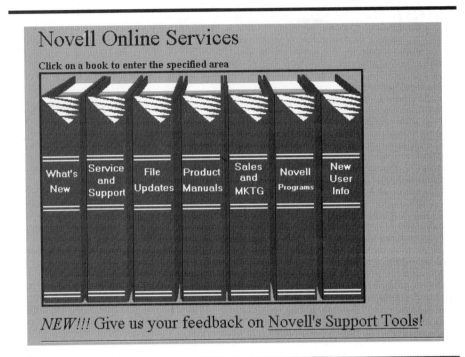

FIGURE 7.3: In the Novell home page you can select the "book" that interests you; click on the book's title and its pages will appear.

What's Out There?

Novell makes volumes of information available at the URL
`http://www.novell.com`.

Small Graphics and Lots of Buttons

Rocket Science uses its home page to promote its product: video games. The page (shown in Figure 7.4) relies on a mixing of text with colorful custom-made graphics to grab your attention. There are plenty of buttons, providing action and also appearing in nice graphical ways. Each graphic is small, however, so it doesn't take long for this page to load.

FIGURE 7.4: The Rocket Science home page is as lively and colorful as a game company's page should be.

What's Out There?

Fly on out to the Rocket Science home page; it's at the URL
`http://www.rocketsci.com`.

A Stately Symmetry

The Welcome to the White House home page (Figure 7.5) uses a large image with hot spots to lead to more information on different pages. This page provides no bureaucratic run-around, it's in a simple (perhaps even *dignified*) symmetrical layout.

What's Out There?

Tour the White House interactively by checking in at the URL
`http://www.whitehouse.gov`.

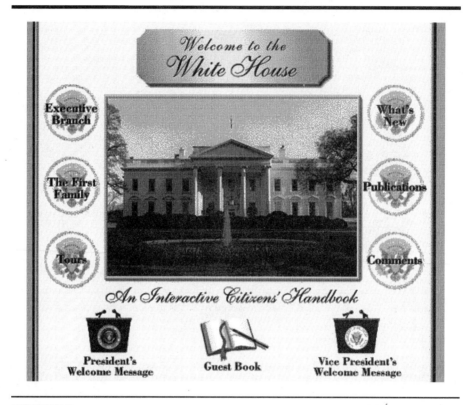

FIGURE 7.5: Welcome to the White House is your entry point to a variety of topics and an electronic tour.

Colorful Graphics as Links

The Internet Underground Music Archive (Figure 7.6) uses lots of small, interesting-looking graphics as links. There are West Coast, East Coast, and European versions of the archive.

What's Out There?

Whether you're a big-time music fan or just a Web wanderer looking for some cool design, check out the Internet Underground Music Archive at the URL `http://www.iuma.com`.

FIGURE 7.6: Take a look (when you get online) at the Internet Underground Music Archive's fun, colorful pages.

File Types and Sizes Identified for Your Convenience

Kevin Hughes is a bona fide Best of the Web hall of famer. We followed links from the Best of the Web page to find his own personal page—a useful exercise, as it turns out, because Kevin's claim to fame is his HTML expertise and innovations. His page illustrates an important point: Kevin provides information on the size and type of each link that goes to a graphic, video, or sound (Figure 7.7).

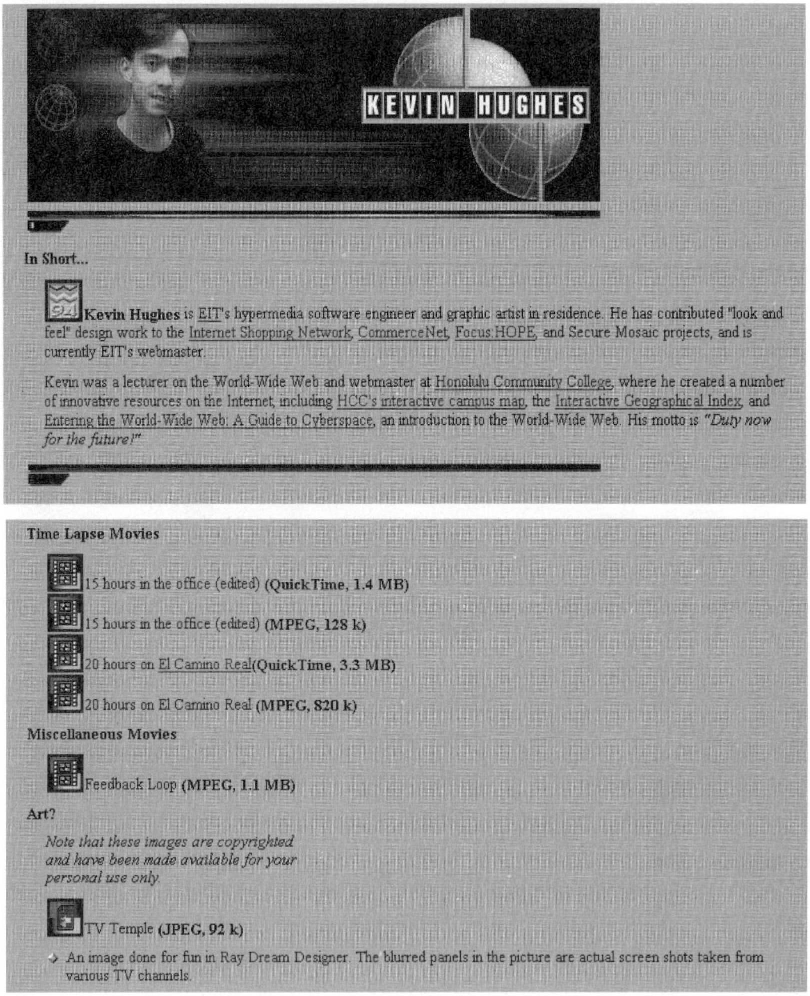

FIGURE 7.7: Kevin Hughes' home page has all the important introductory stuff at the top. If you scroll down the page, you'll find links to video and art, with file types and sizes shown.

What's Out There?

You can see the work of a genuine Web innovator (check out his fancy ruled lines) at the URL `http://www.eit.com/people/kev.html`.

Interactivity at Its Best

One of the most famous and, in our opinions, *best* examples of use of the Web is the interactive frog dissection shown in part in Figure 7.8. The menu in the frog dissection home page lets you choose which phases of the dissection you'd like to see; you can follow the entire process one scene at a time in lifelike color. Of course an added bonus is that millions of people can experience this dissection without killing millions of frogs.

What's Out There?

You can experience a brilliantly innovative interactive frog dissection at the URL
`http:// curry.edschool.virginia.edu/~insttech/frog/menu.html`.

Using HTML to Mark Up a Document

Now let's take a look at how all this is done. Marking up a document is a pretty simple matter of identifying what you want any given element to be and then literally *marking* it as that type of element (Figure 7.9).

The mark up, or commands, in HTML documents are surrounded by angle brackets, like this:

```
<title>
```

These commands usually come in pairs and affect everything between them. For example, surrounding a heading you'll see <h1> at the beginning, matching the </h1> at the end....More on this as we go along.

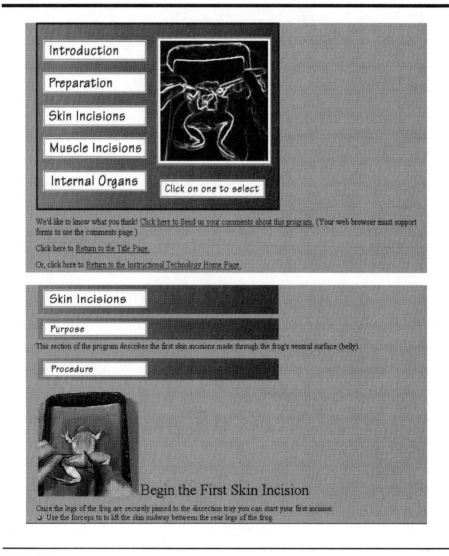

FIGURE 7.8: This interactive frog dissection is one of the best uses of the Web we've ever seen. Bravo!

```
<html>
<head>
<title>10 PM</title>
</head>
<body>
<h1>10 PM</h1>
<h2>by Brenda Kienan</h2>
<p>
        How many women lie in darkness in Quakertown, Lansdale, Perkasie;
considering their pasts, with the undusted rifle rack hanging over the bed and the
green afghan heaped and dragging from the arm of a chair onto the carpet where the
kids pulled it down and went on. Through the drawn shades the sounds of a thousand
crickets and wind sweeping between this trailer and the next. These are the elements
of redemption: the wind rising, rattling the corrugated plastic roof of the neighbor's
carport, the husband coughing over the droning tv news, the washer clicking and
getting louder as the clothes inside it spin out of balance. This is an ordering of events
that carries one day to the next.<p>
        How many women, each in her own separate darkness, surveying what might
have happened, while the rushing wind finds its way into heating ducts and whistles
through tin.<p>
        <i>Papa, it is vanishing.</i> The blue June evenings and the scent of dusty
pavement as a long-awaited rain falls. <i>I thought I'd still know, but I'm
drifting.</i> White tulips. Gold star confetti sprayed across starched tablecloths.
The priest's thick fingers holding a book.<p>
        How many women making a list, of the ways they might have gone, of the
friends they see in markets, marriages lost, pushing carts full of children, sugary
cereals, cheap meats. How many mornings of driving: her own child to another's care,
her husband (who's lost his license) to work, herds of teenagers in a yellow bus to
school. How many times the red-haired boy pushing his way to the seat behind her,
bringing her gifts of novelty pencils, a sandwich, cloisonn&eacute; earrings.<p>
        How many women wondering, each in her cool separate darkness, if the news
is yet over, if the wind will grow still.<p>
<h3>Copyright 1995 Brenda Kienan</h3>
</body>
</html>
```

10 PM

by Brenda Kienan

How many women lie in darkness in Quakertown, Lansdale, Perkasie; considering their pasts, with the undusted rifle rack hanging over the bed and the green afghan heaped and dragging from the arm of a chair onto the carpet where the kids pulled it down and went on. Through the drawn shades the sounds of a thousand crickets and wind sweeping between this trailer and the next. These are the elements of redemption: the wind rising, rattling the corrugated plastic roof of the neighbor's carport, the husband coughing over the droning tv news, the washer clicking and getting louder as the clothes inside it spin out of balance. This is an ordering of events that carries one day to the next.

How many women, each in her own separate darkness, surveying what might have happened, while the rushing wind finds its way into heating ducts and whistles through tin.

Papa, it is vanishing. The blue June evenings and the scent of dusty pavement as a long-awaited rain falls. *I thought I'd still know, but I'm drifting.* White tulips. Gold star confetti sprayed across starched tablecloths. The priest's thick fingers holding a book.

How many women making a list, of the ways they might have gone, of the friends they see in markets, marriages lost, pushing carts full of children, sugary cereals, cheap meats. How many mornings of driving: her own child to another's care, her husband (who's lost his license) to work, herds of teenagers in a yellow bus to school. How many times the red-haired boy pushing his way to the seat behind her, bringing her gifts of novelty pencils, a sandwich, cloisonné earrings.

How many women wondering, each in her cool separate darkness, if the news is yet over, if the wind will grow still.

Copyright 1995 Brenda Kienan

FIGURE 7.9: In an HTML-coded document (above) you see commands (within angle brackets) surrounding the element to which they refer. In the resulting Web document (below), you do not see the commands—you see only the effect they have on the document displayed.

One major exception to the pairing of HTML commands can be found in the New Paragraph command, which stands alone at the beginning of a new paragraph.

In Figure 7.10 you'll see all the elements of a basic HTML document and how it turned out when viewed on the Web with Air Mosaic. Take note of:

◆ The entire document enclosed between `<html>` and `</html>`

◆ The title of the document enclosed between `<title>` and `</title>`

◆ The header of the document enclosed between `<h1>` and `</h1>`

◆ The body of the document enclosed between `<body>` and `</body>`

In the sections that follow, we'll look at the basic HTML commands you can use in your documents. Remember as we go along that these commands are the same whether you are marking up a document in a word processor or in an HTML editor.

 If you're using a word processor to create an original document you intend for Web publication, you can of course simply write in the HTML coding as you go along; you don't have to write the document first and convert it later.

```
<HTML>                                              ──────── Beginning of document
<TITLE>The Page's Title Goes Here</TITLE>  ──────── Title
<H1>The Page's Title Is Usually Repeated Here</H1>── Header
<BODY>
Here is the body of the page.              ──────── Body of document
</BODY>
</HTML>                                             ──────── End of document
```

FIGURE 7.10: Here you can see the HTML coding for the most basic elements of a Web document.

Every Document Must Have the "Required" Commands

Every HTML document must include certain commands, which essentially identify the document as an HTML document and as such, show its beginning and end. Note that even these most fundamental HTML commands come in pairs—the <html> at the beginning of the documents matches the </html> at the end of the document.

Marking Up Heads

HTML supports six levels of heads. Each level of head will look different when it's displayed in a Web browser like Air Mosaic. The highest level (let's call this the "1" head) will be larger and more obvious, the lowest level (the "6" head) will be smallest and most discreet.

 The actual way each head looks is different from one browser to the next. In other words, HTML allows you to say what text is a head, but not what the head will look like when User A accesses it with Air Mosaic, User B with NCSA Mosaic, and User C with Netscape or Cello.

The text of the head should appear between two head codes <h*n*> and </h*n*>, where *n* can be any number between 1 and 6. It is customary to start your document with a level 1 head, to indicate the important topic that comes first in your document. You can follow a level 1 head with heads of lower levels; you can also place new level 1 heads further down in your document, as you please.

Beginning New Paragraphs

You must explicitly code each and every new paragraph of text by placing the <p> code at its beginning. You needn't close a paragraph with any coding, however—as noted previously, this new paragraph business is one of the major exceptions to the "opening and closing" paired codes that are the general rule in HTML.

 Web browsers will not start a new paragraph at any place that does not include the <p> code, regardless of how your document looks in your word processor.

Inserting Ruled Lines

Rules, or ruled lines, are horizontal lines that you can use to separate parts of your document. To place a rule in your document, use the <HR> command. (See Figure 7.11.) Again, it is unnecessary to indicate the end of the rule with a closing code. The ruled line you code in to your document will cross the Web page (whatever size the page is on screen) from the left margin to the right.

```
We now have an on-line <A HREF="http://www.sybex.com/catalog.html">catalog</A>
<HR>
Thanks for visiting!
```

We now have an on-line catalog

Thanks for visiting!

FIGURE 7.11: The coding you see in the HTML document (above) results in the rule you see in the Web document (below).

Creating Lists

You can have two types of lists in a Web document: numbered and bulleted. In HTML lingo, numbered lists are called *ordered* lists and bulleted lists are called *unordered* lists.

Ordered Lists

Ordered (numbered) lists will be the result of text nested between the <OL> and </OL> codes. Each new item in the ordered list must start with the <LI> code. Unlike most other HTML codes, the <LI> code need not be ended with a </LI> code. For example, a numbered list of types of fruit would look like:

```
<OL>
<LI>Apple
<LI>Orange
<LI>Cherry
</OL>
```

A Web browser would display the above list like:

1. Apple

2. Orange

3. Cherry

 When you're coding an ordered list, you need not enter the numbers. The HTML coding tells the Web browser to number the items sequentially in the order in which they appear.

Unordered Lists

Unordered (bulleted) lists will be the result of text nested between the <UL> and </UL> codes. This, of course, is very similar to what you do to create an ordered list. Each new item in the bulleted list must begin with a <LI> code. This is *exactly* like what you do with each item in an ordered list; it is the 0 or U in the opening and closing codes that "tell" whether the list is to be numbered or bulleted—and again, you need not be bothered with placing any type of bullets. They will appear when the document is viewed on screen wherever you have placed the <LI> code in your unordered list.

 Remember that the bullets will look different and be of different sizes in the different Web browsers various users have.

Creating Links

Now we get to the heart of things. As you know well by now, the beauty of the Web is the way documents are inter-related through being linked to each other—that's what makes the Web so wonderfully webby. Let's take a look behind the scenes at the HTML underpinnings of a link.

In HTML lingo, a link is really what's called an *anchor*, the opening code for which is <A. What the anchor looks like when it appears as a link in a Web document will differ depending on which Web browser is being used, but usually it'll show up as underlined blue text. When you click on the link (the underlined blue text) the underlying anchor is activated, and the file it is associated with (the other end of the link, if you will) is loaded and displayed on screen.

Here's an example of how this works in HTML: if you wanted the word <u>Catalog</u> to appear in a document as a hot link, you'd code the word like this:

```
<A HREF = "http://www.sybex.com/catalog.html">Catalog</A>
```

Then, when the document is viewed with any Web browser, such as Air Mosaic, the word <u>Catalog</u> will appear as a hot link. When a user clicks on it, the file CATALOG.HTML will automatically be transferred from the HTTP server `www.sybex.com`, and Sybex's catalog will appear on screen.

Creating Links to Sound and Movies

In your Web roamings, you've probably found links that go not to HTML documents, but perhaps instead to graphics, sounds, and videos. The URL in a link doesn't have to point to another HTML document; it can point to any type of file. For example, the anchor

```
<A HREF = "http://www.iuma.com/IUMA/ftp/music/Madonna/
Secret.mpg">Madonna</A>
```

creates a link to the machine `www.iuma.com`, where a video clip from Madonna's Secret video is stored. When you click on the link, the video will be transferred to your computer and a player for MPEG files will start up so you can see the video—the trigger for that action is in the HTML coding shown above. You can create links to any type of file in this manner—just include in the URL the full path to the file.

Remember, you must indicate the type of file to which you are linking; this will "tell" the Web browser employed by any given user how to deal with the file. When it comes to images, most Web browsers "out of the box" can deal only with GIF and XBM files. You'll need special viewers (as described in Chapter 8) to view images or play sounds in other file formats.

Creating Glossaries

A *glossary* in a Web document is a special element designed to let you place definitions in your documents. Glossaries look a bit like lists when they are coded with HTML; the list of these items must be surrounded by the codes <DL> and </DL>. Each defined *term* in the glossary starts with the code <DT>. The definition itself follows the term it applies to, and begins with the code <DD>. Neither <DT> or <DD> codes need closing codes.

Here is a sample of coding for a glossary:

```
<DL>
<DT>Apple
<DD>A round fruit, often red in color when ripe but some-
times green
<DT>Orange
<DD>A round, orange fruit
<DT>Cherry
<DD>A small, round, red fruit
</DL>
```

The result of this sample coding will look like this:

> Apple
>   A round fruit, often red in color when ripe but sometimes green
> Orange
>   A round, orange fruit
> Cherry
>   A small, round, red fruit

Inserting Addresses

Address is a special HTML element that was originally designed to hold the address of the author of the page. (The snail-mail address, the e-mail address,

or both.) Most Web browsers display this element in an italic font, smaller than body text. For example,

```
<ADDRESS>
Daniel A. Tauber and Brenda Kienan
<P>Sybex
<P>2021 Challenger Drive
<P>Alameda, CA 94501
</ADDRESS>
```

will appear as shown here:

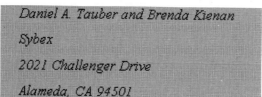

Assigning Text Attributes: Bold, Italic, and Underline

You are probably familiar with *text attributes* from word processors—things like bold, italic, and character color, which differentiate some text from the usual, are all known as *attributes* in a word processor. You can specify attributes such as these using HTML.

 Remember that none of the formatting or text attributes you might have in your word processed document will carry over to your Web document—you must specify what you want using HTML coding.

The types of attributes you can specify using HTML are broken down into two classes:

◆ Physical

◆ Logical

The *physical* attributes specify how text characters should look: italic or bold, for example. They will be italic or bold no matter which Web browser is used for viewing. The *logical* attributes specify the amount of emphasis you want to give to important text; you can choose to make text *emphasized* or *strongly emphasized*. In many cases, this will turn out to be just italic or bold, but some Web browsers will have different ways of showing logical attributes. (Maybe strongly emphasized text will be red, or in a slightly larger size, for example.) The choice of using logical or physical attributes is yours. Some people prefer to use physical attributes because they want to control the way the text finally looks. Other people prefer to use logical attributes because they convey "meaning" without specifying what the text should look like.

HTML attribute commands must appear in pairs—the first code turns the attribute on and the last one turns it off.

Physical Attributes

You can use physical attributes to make text appear bold, italic, or underlined. (Color, unfortunately, is not an attribute that is available in Mosaic.)

The underline attribute is not the same as the underlining that appears under hot links—Air Mosaic generates the hot link underline automatically when you code for a link.

The codes used to apply these attributes are summarized here:

To Get This Attribute	Use the Starting Code	And the Ending Code
Bold	\<B\>	\</B\>
Italic	\<I\>	\</I\>
<u>Underline</u>	\<U\>	\</U\>

You can embed attributes within other attributes. Just make sure the opening code that's first-in corresponds to the closing code that's last-out. For example, to make the phrase Bungee Jumping both bold and italic, use the coding `<B><I>Bungee Jumping</I></B>`.

Logical Attributes

You can use logical attributes to give emphasis or strong emphasis to text you feel is important. The way the text actually appears when viewed in a browser depends on the browser's individual way of handling these attributes. The logical attributes that you can use are:

To Get This Attribute	Use the Starting Code	And the Ending Code
Emphasis	`<EM>`	`</EM>`
Strong Emphasis	`<STRONG>`	`</STRONG>`

Here you can see the result of making text emphasized and strongly emphasized and then viewing the text with Air Mosaic:

Emphasis and **Strong Emphasis**

Using Special Characters

Some special characters are available in HTML. For example, you'll often want to use the special character for the copyright symbol (©). But HTML files are really plain text files, so you don't have access to some other special characters: an unfortunate example is the symbol that's used to indicate copyright for digital audio, a letter P enclosed in a circle.

Some "special" characters you'd use fairly regularly in word-processed text, such as the angle brackets and ampersand, have special meanings in HTML, as you know if you've read earlier sections of this chapter. To include characters such as these in your HTML document, you'll have to insert special escape codes for them in your file. Here are some examples:

For the Symbol	Which Means	Use the Code
&	Ampersand	&amp;
>	Less Than	&lt;
<	Greater Than	&gt;

What's Out There?

You can get a complete list of special characters and how to code for them at the URL
`http://info.cern.ch/hypertext/WWW/MarkUp/ISOlat1.html`.

Embedding Images

Images that appear as part of a Web page are called *inline images*. While it is possible to place many, many inline images in your document, remember that including them can greatly increase the time required to load and view the document.

It's best in some circumstances to place thumbnails of images in your page—thumbnails load a lot faster than larger images—and link the thumbnail to the larger image, allowing users to download the bigger image if they want to and have time to wait for it. See <u>Mixing Elements</u> on the next page.

Any image that you want to include as an inline image in a Web document must be in one of two graphics file formats: GIF or XBM. XBM is a Unix image format, and this, of course, is a Windows book, so let's look more closely at use of the GIF format in this section.

Some enhanced Web browsers (including Air Mosaic) can display inline images in JPEG format. JPEG files are much smaller in size than other image files so they appear on screen much more quickly—a real advantage. The drawback, however, is that not all Web browsers can display them. If you use JPEG and a user tries viewing your document with a browser that can't handle JPEG, all he or she will see is a little error message where the image should be.

You can use the <IMG> command to place an inline image into your HTML document. For example,

```
<IMG SRC="http://www.sybex.com/covers/1327.gif">
```

will cause the image stored in the file 1327.GIF in the directory COVERS on the machine www.sybex.com to be displayed as part of the Web document.

What's Out There?

You can scope out a helpful Scanning FAQ for extensive tips on scanning images to use in yoiur Web documents. To find the Scanning FAQ, use http://www.dopig.uab.edu/dopigpages/FAQ/The-Scan-FAQ.html. Transparent GIFs are GIFs in which one of the colors is invisible. (you might want to do this if you'd like the background color the user's Mosaic is using to be one of the colors in the image.) To reveal how yiu can make your GIFs transparent, look into the URL http://melmac.harris-atd.com/transparent_images.html.

● Mixing Elements

Just as you can create bold-italic text by embedding the italic code within the bold code, you can embed one type of HTML element within another element. For example, you might want to create an unordered (bulleted) list in which each element is a hot link to another Web page. In fact, if you think about it, your entire HTML file is embedded between the <html> and </html> commands, so everything in your document is already embedded between two standard HTML commands.

Another practical use for embedded HTML commands is as a link that leads to an image. In that case, the inline image command is embedded inside the link command. (And this, dear reader, takes us to the next section.)

Using Pictures as Links

To make an image act as a hot link to another document, you can use the link command, <A, followed by indicators of what you're linking to, followed by </A>. In a nutshell, here's what you do: where you'd normally place the text the user will click on to activate the link, you instead place the command to display an inline image. For example, if you have an image called TOCATALOG.GIF, you could place

```
<A HREF="http://www.sybex.com/catalog.html"><IMG
src="http://www.sybex.com/tocatalog.gif"></IMG></A>
```

in your Web document to create a link to the page stored in the file CATA-LOG.HTML. This causes the Web browser to display the image TOCATA-LOG.GIF with a blue border around it. When a user clicks anywhere in the picture the link will become activated, and in this case, the Catalog page indicated will appear.

Creating Lists of Links

Let's say you want a list of links. To do this, create an ordered or unordered list, placing a link as each item in the list. For example,

```
<UL>
<LI><A HREF="http://www.sybex.com/sybex.html">Sybex's Home
Page</A>
<LI><A HREF="http://www.sybex.com/catalog.html">Sybex's
Catalog</A>
<LI><A HREF="http://www.sybex.com/people/dan.html">My Home
Page</A>
</UL>
```

produces a bulleted list with three items, each of which is a link to another page:

- Sybex's Home Page
- Sybex's Catalog
- My Home Page

Creating a Simple Home Page

Great. Now, having read this chapter, you know all the HTML commands that go into creating a simple page. Let's go step-by-step through creating a home page. We'll use Word for Windows to do this, and when we're done, we'll save the file as a plain text file.

To follow along, start up Word for Windows and open a new, empty document window.

 Just about everything we do here you can do in any word processor. If you use a different word processor—Ami Pro or WordPerfect, for example—you can follow along, substituting as necessary the functions and commands your word processor uses.

1. In your blank, new document window, type **<html>** and press ⏎ to start your page. (Remember that all HTML documents should be surrounded by the <html> and </html> commands. We'll put in the </html> later, at the end of these steps.)

2. Now type **<title>Herkimer Uglyface's Home Page</title>** and press ⏎. (You can replace Herkimer Uglyface with your own name, which is probably more attractive, anyway.) This will make the title of your home page appear in the title bar when your page is viewed by a user.

3. Now type **<h1>Herkimer Uglyface's Home Page</h1>** and press ⏎. This will make the title of your home page appear at the top of your home page. (Although it's customary to use the same text for the title and the first head, you can actually enter whatever you want in place of "Herkimer Uglyface's Home Page" here.)

4. Now we are ready to enter some body text, so type **<body>** and press ⏎. This will tell the Web browser that what follows is the body text of the document.

5. Type in a few paragraphs of body text. Remember as you do this to use the **<p>** command at the beginning of every new paragraph.

6. If you want people viewing your page to reach you by e-mail, you can add a link to your e-mail address. Type **<A HREF="mailto:** followed immediately by your e-mail address (with no space after `mailto:`). After your e-mail address (again no space should follow the address), type **">You can send me e-mail.</A>**. (Don't type that last period. It's only there to make our editor happy.) Press ↵.

7. Once you have typed the body text for your page, and added your e-mail link if you chose to, type **</body>** to end the body text and **</html>** to end the document. These two HTML commands match their counterparts at the beginning of the document. You can press ↵ after each of these commands, but it's not necessary.

Now it's time to save the document. (Remember, we're using Word for Windows for this demo.)

1. From the Word for Windows menu bar, select File ➤ Save As. The Save As dialog box will appear.

2. In the Save As dialog box, click on the down arrow next to the text box labeled Save File As Type. A list of file types recognized by Word for Windows will appear. From this list, select Text Only (Figure 7.12).

FIGURE 7.12:   In the list of file types, select Text Only.

3. Type in a path and filename for the file in the File Name text box. If you're saving the file to your hard disk, and placing it in your Mosaic directory, the path will probably be C:\SPRY. You're stuck with the DOS file-naming conventions in naming your file—eight characters only. Our hero, Herkimer Uglyface, named his file HERKPAGE.HTM—you'll have to end the file with the extension .HTM, because this is an HTML file you are saving.

4. Click on the OK button to save the file.

When Word for Windows is finished saving the file, the Save As dialog box will close automatically. You can now exit Word for Windows. Don't be alarmed if Word for Windows asks if you want to save changes to your file when you exit even though you just saved the file as a text file. Just answer No and continue to exit Word for Windows.

 Don't answer Yes, if Word for Windows asks if you want to save changes to your file when you exit after having saved the file as a text file; if you do, Word for Windows will overwrite your text file with a Word file.

Good work. We're ready to look at the file with Air Mosaic to see how it turned out.

Using Air Mosaic to Check Your HTML Document

You've created an HTML document and saved it as a text file on your hard disk. Before you make your page public, you'll want to test it. You can use Air Mosaic to see what your finely crafted page will look like when it's viewed with a Web browser (in this case, Air Mosaic). To load a file from your hard disk into Air Mosaic, follow these steps:

1. Start Air Mosaic and select File ➤ Open Local File from the menu bar. The Open File dialog box will appear.

2. In the Open Local File dialog box, highlight the filename you gave your page. (The Open File dialog box works here just as it does in any Windows application.) Click on the OK button.

3. The dialog box will close, and in a few seconds your home page will appear on screen, in the form of a beautiful Web document!

You won't be able to fix typos or other errors or add things to your HTML document while you are viewing it with Air Mosaic. If you want to make changes, close Air Mosaic, open up your word processor, and make the changes there. Then, you can save the modified file, and re-open it in Air Mosaic to see the changes you just made.

Making Your HTML Document Available to the World

Having created a wonderful HTML document on your own computer, you'll want to make it available to the world. As a Web publisher, you can, if you have a big pile of money, buy a machine and set it up as a Web server. This is simply not practical for most people, so we're going to skip it. You can also, if you have access to a Web server at a university or elsewhere, sneak your page onto that server (but don't say we said so). A third option, more practical for a lot of people, might be to publish your page with the help of your Internet service provider. (This is assuming you have an account with a general-purpose provider in addition to your specialized Spry Mosaic/CompuServe account.) Unfortunately, this is sometimes not free—check with your service provider about costs, and if there is an unreasonable charge, *switch providers*.

Some companies, like Web Communications, will rent you space on their server. If you don't have an account with a general-purpose provider in addition to your specialized Spry Mosaic/CompuServe account, this may be a good option. The URL for Web Communications is http//www/webcom.com.

The technical specifics of making your Web pages available to the world also vary from one Internet service provider to another, so we cannot go into *great* detail in this book. Contact your service provider to see how they recommend you make your documents available to the Internet public.

For your HTML documents to become available to the world, they must be stored on an FTP or HTTP *server* computer that is connected to the Internet. This, for all practical purposes, is not going to be your stand-alone PC with a dial-up connection to the Internet. It'll be a specially outfitted computer that belongs to your Internet service provider. They'll tell you how to transfer your files to their machine and what URLs people should use to access your page.

When Your Page Is Ready, Publicize It

One of the worst tragedies in publishing of any sort is a wonderful piece of work that goes unnoticed because *nobody knows it's there.* Don't let this happen to your Web page. Sure, some people are bound to stumble across it; but you probably want lots and *lots* of people to see it—otherwise, why publish it on the Net?

Take a lesson from the experience of others: when Enterzone, the literary rag mentioned in Chapter 5 of this book, went "live" in late '94, it got only about 20 hits a day until it was listed in the NCSA What's New page— after that listing, Enterzone's hits per day increased a hundredfold. We've heard the anecdote, too, of *Virtual Vegas*, an experimental "virtual trade show booth" that went from a few dozen hits per day to tens of thousands after being listed. (*Virtual Vegas* also benefited from a short, catchy title with all the implied glitz of the casinos.)

 The NCSA What's New document is visited by over 3 million users per week. We discuss it in detail in Chapters 4 and 5; its URL (for your reference one more time) is
`http://www.ncsa.uiuc.edu/SDG/Software/`
`Mosaic/Docs/whats-new.html.`

Another venue for announcing your page might be various carefully selected Usenet newsgroups. Choose appropriate newsgroups based on whether their topics are related to the topic of your page.

You can also announce your page via Internet mailing lists like Net-Happenings. To subscribe to Net-Happenings, send e-mail to `listserv@is.internic.net`; in the body of your message, type: **subscribe net-happenings** and add your full name.

You can also <u>trade links</u> with others who've published pages on related topics (or even unrelated topics).

If your page is of a *commercial* nature, you can list it for free along with over 800 other companies in Open Market's Commercial Sites Index.

What's Out There?

Open Market's Commercial Sites Index can be found at the URL `http://www.directory.net/`.

What's Next?

Well. Now you know all you need to know to browse the Web, search for what you find intriguing or useful, and create your own home page. In the rest of this book, we're going to show you how to get some nifty viewers from the Internet itself and then we'll cover the nitty-gritty technical details of how to install and set up Spry's Air Mosaic.

Getting and Installing Video Viewers and Sound Players

In your Web travels you've probably come across pages that include links to video and sound clips. You can click on these links to view little movies (Figure 8.1) or play sounds. We've been warning you throughout this book that the files for video and sound are really big, and that to experience the video or sound, you need external *viewers*. Viewers are special programs that enable Air Mosaic to handle the video or sound files—really, they're just Windows programs that Air Mosaic calls upon to "display" files it cannot display itself.

In this chapter we're going to cover downloading (getting), installing, and using the most useful viewers—with these viewers and Spry's Air Mosaic in your tool kit, you'll be ready to handle video and sound when you encounter it on the Web.

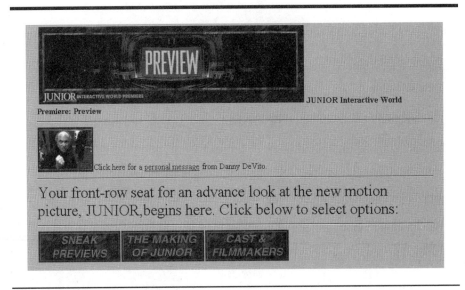

FIGURE 8.1: Stars are interviewed and trailers are shown in an online premiere of a Hollywood movie.

  Just a reminder: video and sound are very exciting additions to the Web, but the files for video and sound take eons to travel over a phone line to your machine. Even with the correct viewers, be prepared to wait around a while, and make sure you have enough memory and disk storage on your machine to cope with the big files.

What's Out There?

This has nothing to do with viewers, really, but you can find a giant archive of Windows programs and other files at the Center for Innovative Computer Applications' FTP server at
`ftp://ftp.cica.indiana.edu/pub/pc/win3`.
There's some really useful stuff there, so check it out.

What's Available

A number of viewers are available; to pump Air Mosaic up to its best capacity, you might want a video viewer that can handle movies in QuickTime format (with the extension .MOV) and the MPEG format (.MPG, .MPEG, or .MPE), and a sound "viewer" (or *player*) that lets you play files in Sun Audio format (with the extension .AU) as well as Windows sound files (.WAV) and Macintosh sound files (.SND).

What's Out There?

NCSA maintains a listing of viewers that work with Mosaic—the information on the page is somewhat biased toward NCSA Mosaic, but you can use all of the listed viewers with your copy of Air Mosaic. The URL for NCSA's page listing viewers is
`http://www.ncsa.uiuc.edu/SDG/Software/WinMosaic/viewers.html.`

Video and Air Mosaic

The two most popular formats for video on the Web are QuickTime, developed by Apple Computer, and MPEG, developed by the Motion Picture Expert Group. It is important to note that while QuickTime was developed by Apple, any video that has the QuickTime `.mov` extension can be played by any machine that has the correct viewer (the one that works for that machine). In other words, you can play a QuickTime video clip on your PC, even if it was developed on a Mac, as long as you have a QuickTime viewer on your PC.

Functionally, MPEG is very similar to QuickTime—however, MPEG was developed by the Motion Picture Expert Group (hence, the acronym MPEG), a fine group of people who made MPEG available free of charge.

Getting and Setting Up
the QuickTime Viewer

To view QuickTime video, files with the extension .MOV, you need a QuickTime viewer that works with Air Mosaic. Let's take a look at how to

Compression Makes Video on the Internet a Reality

The big breakthrough that made it possible for users to create, transfer, and view video clips was *compression*. Simply put, there was technology available a while ago that let people create electronic videos, but there was a problem, which was that the files for video were so *outrageously* huge that even souped-up machines couldn't store them, no floppy disk could contain them, and transferring them over a modem would take (no joke) *days*. It's an interesting aside in our discussion of video on the Net that QuickTime and MPEG are not software products that let you shoot little movies, they are actually *compression* technologies that take the enormous files containing little movies, and shrink them adequately so they can be stored and transferred with a minimum of hassle.

This is not like *zipping* files—that's a process that crunches data into a smaller storage space—this type of compression involves sacrificing or losing some of the less important data. Not much, mind you—if you imagine an animated sequence that is very smooth, because it has many, many frames of action, and another that's just a bit choppy because some of the frames were left out, you can understand the acceptable "lossiness" of compressed video.

Now here's the difference between QuickTime and MPEG: QuickTime was developed for commercial distribution as a software product and MPEG was developed as a technology anyone can use. You'll see lots of Quick-Time video files on the Web and some MPEG files. It's best to have a viewer for each product in your Air Mosaic tool kit.

get such a viewer, how to install it, and how to set it up to work neatly with Air Mosaic.

Downloading the QuickTime Viewer

Before you can view QuickTime video with Air Mosaic, you must *download* (transfer to your system) the correct software. Here's how:

1. With Air Mosaic running, select File ➤ Open URL from the menu bar. The Open URL dialog box will appear.

2. In the Open URL dialog box's text box, type **ftp://ftp.ncsa.uiuc.edu/Mosaic/Windows/viewers**. In a few seconds, the contents of a directory of viewers will appear in the form of a Web page with a link for each viewer (Figure 8.2).

The site `ftp.ncsa.uiuc.edu` is terrifically popular—so much so that it sometimes rejects new connections. If you try to load the viewers list and your connection is rejected, try, try again. (Try off hours, especially.)

3. Scroll down the page until you see the link labeled qtw11.zip; shift-click on that link. The Save As dialog box will appear.

4. In the Save As dialog box's File Name text box, type **c:\qtw11.zip**.

5. Now click on the OK button to start downloading the QuickTime viewer software to your computer.

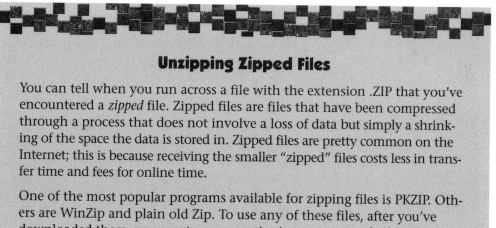

Unzipping Zipped Files

You can tell when you run across a file with the extension .ZIP that you've encountered a *zipped* file. Zipped files are files that have been compressed through a process that does not involve a loss of data but simply a shrinking of the space the data is stored in. Zipped files are pretty common on the Internet; this is because receiving the smaller "zipped" files costs less in transfer time and fees for online time.

One of the most popular programs available for zipping files is PKZIP. Others are WinZip and plain old Zip. To use any of these files, after you've downloaded them, you must use an unzipping program, which will expand the files to the size they were before they were zipped. To unzip files, you can use PKUNZIP, the unzip feature in WinZip, or the freely available program UNZIP. Here's the best thing: you can get Zip and UnZip from the Internet. They're available at the FTP site `ftp.oak.oakland.edu`, as well as from the Sybex CompuServe forum and scores of other sites.

(continued on next page)

(continued from previous page)

To get a copy of Zip and UnZip from `ftp.oak.oakland.edu` using Air Mosaic:

1. Start Air Mosaic, and from the menu bar, select Options ➤ Load To Disk Mode. This toggles on Load To Disk Mode, telling Air Mosaic to *save* whatever you transfer to your hard disk instead of displaying it on screen.

2. Now select File ➤ Open URL from Air Mosaic's menu bar. The Open URL dialog box will appear. You've seen this dialog box often in earlier parts of this book.

3. In the Open URL dialog box's text box, type **ftp://oak.oakland.edu/pub/msdos/UNZIP.EXE**. (When you do this, pay attention to the capitalization.) In a few seconds, the familiar Windows-style Save As dialog box will appear, asking you exactly where on your hard disk you want to save the file you are transferring to your machine.

4. Select the directory C:\DOS as your choice of storage location and click on OK.

5. Now select Options ➤ Load To Disk Mode from Air Mosaic's menu bar to toggle off and disable Load To Disk Mode.

The file UNZIP.EXE will be copied to the DOS directory on your computer. The progress of copying files will be shown in the status bar along the bottom of the window. When it's finished, you'll be ready to unzip zipped files—like the ones that contain viewers you can use with Air Mosaic.

You can follow the progress of your transfer—its status will be shown in the status bar along the bottom of the window. When the file transfer is complete, you're all set to install the QuickTime viewer. Close Air Mosaic by selecting File ➤ Exit from the menu bar.

Transferring a file is not the same as installing the software contained in the file. When you transfer the file, you are simply moving the (presumably) zipped file from its location elsewhere to your machine, where it is simply stored until you unzip it and actually <u>install</u> the software. Installing software these days is usually a pretty simple process—a lot of software installs itself by checking out your machine and what's already on it, then fitting itself in, and making necessary adjustments along the way.

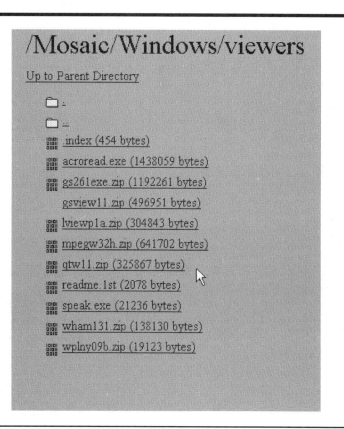

FIGURE 8.2: A directory of viewers in the form of a Web page; click on the link for the viewer that interests you.

Installing the QuickTime Viewer

Now, with the QuickTime viewer file transferred to your machine, it's time to unzip the thing and install the software on your hard disk. Here's how:

1. Beginning in the Windows Program Manager's Main group, get yourself to the DOS prompt by double-clicking on the MS-DOS icon.

MS-DOS
Prompt

You should find yourself in the WINDOWS directory, so the prompt will look something like C:\WINDOWS.

2. Now type **cd \windows\system**; this will get you into the C:\WINDOWS\SYSTEM directory, which is where the QuickTime viewer file must be stored.

3. Type **unzip \qtw11.zip** to unzip the zipped files that make up the QuickTime viewer. As files are unzipped, their names will appear along with their size and a few other details that are of no concern to us here. When unzipping is complete, the DOS prompt (C:\WINDOWS\SYSTEM) will appear again on screen.

4. Type **exit** to return to Windows. The Program Manager's Main group will reappear.

Next order of business: you'll have to modify two of the Windows initialization files in order for the viewer to work correctly. Not to worry; this sounds more technically difficult than it is.

5. From the Windows Program Manager's menu, select File ➤ Run. The Run dialog box will appear.

6. In the Run dialog box's Command Line text box, type **notepad c:\windows\win.ini**. Click on the OK button. The Run dialog box will be replaced by a Notepad window (Figure 8.3). Notepad is a simple text editor that comes with Windows.

Windows configuration files like WIN.INI and SYSTEM.INI are divided into a number of *sections*. You don't need to worry about this—each section has to do with a different part of Windows, but there's no need to concern yourself with that information to do this process. Just keep in mind that each section will appear in the Notepad window with the name of the section surrounded by square brackets, like this: [Printers].

7. Look for [extensions] and under it, type **mov=mplayer.exe /play ^.mov**, then press ↵.

8. Look for [mci.extensions] and under it, type **mov=QTWVideo**, then press ↵.

9. Select File ➤ Save to save the changes you just made.

10. Select File ➤ Open and the Open dialog box will appear.

11. Type **\windows\system.ini** into the File Name box and click on the OK button. Notepad will load the file SYSTEM.INI into the Notepad window (Figure 8.4).

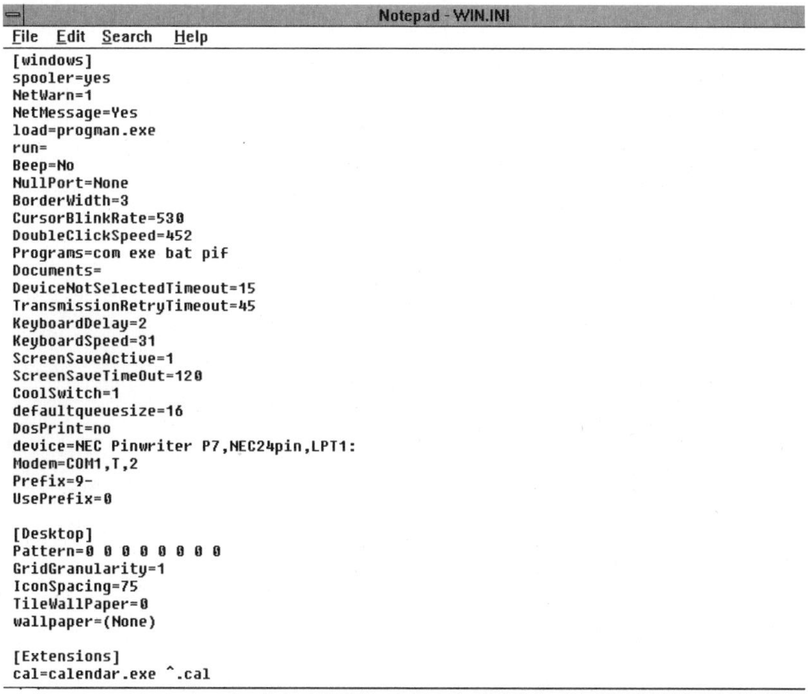

```
┌─────────────────── Notepad - WIN.INI ───────────────────┐
│ File  Edit  Search  Help                                 │
│ [windows]                                                │
│ spooler=yes                                              │
│ NetWarn=1                                                │
│ NetMessage=Yes                                           │
│ load=progman.exe                                         │
│ run=                                                     │
│ Beep=No                                                  │
│ NullPort=None                                            │
│ BorderWidth=3                                            │
│ CursorBlinkRate=530                                      │
│ DoubleClickSpeed=452                                     │
│ Programs=com exe bat pif                                 │
│ Documents=                                               │
│ DeviceNotSelectedTimeout=15                              │
│ TransmissionRetryTimeout=45                              │
│ KeyboardDelay=2                                          │
│ KeyboardSpeed=31                                         │
│ ScreenSaveActive=1                                       │
│ ScreenSaveTimeOut=120                                    │
│ CoolSwitch=1                                             │
│ defaultqueuesize=16                                      │
│ DosPrint=no                                              │
│ device=NEC Pinwriter P7,NEC24pin,LPT1:                   │
│ Modem=COM1,T,2                                           │
│ Prefix=9-                                                │
│ UsePrefix=0                                              │
│                                                          │
│ [Desktop]                                                │
│ Pattern=0 0 0 0 0 0 0                                    │
│ GridGranularity=1                                        │
│ IconSpacing=75                                           │
│ TileWallPaper=0                                          │
│ wallpaper=(None)                                         │
│                                                          │
│ [Extensions]                                             │
│ cal=calendar.exe ^.cal                                   │
└──────────────────────────────────────────────────────────┘
```

FIGURE 8.3: Notepad is a simple text editor.

12. Look for [mci] and under it, type **QTWVideo=mciqtw.drv**, then press ↵.

13. Select File ➤ Save from the menu bar. The changes you just made in the file will be saved.

14. From Notepad's menu bar, select File ➤ Exit to return to Windows.

15. Now exit Windows by selecting File ➤ Exit Windows from the Program Manager's menu bar. The DOS prompt will appear (something like C:\.)

16. Restart Windows by typing **win** and pressing ↵. The changes you made will now take effect.

Now let's set up Air Mosaic so it will automatically call upon the viewer you've installed whenever it encounters QuickTime files.

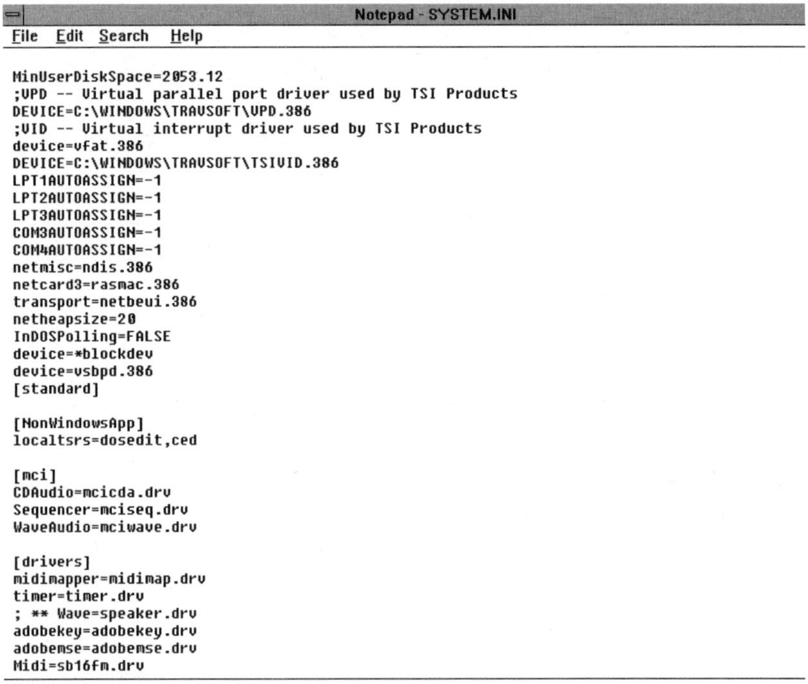

```
┌─                         Notepad - SYSTEM.INI
 File   Edit   Search   Help

MinUserDiskSpace=2053.12
;UPD -- Virtual parallel port driver used by TSI Products
DEVICE=C:\WINDOWS\TRAVSOFT\VPD.386
;VID -- Virtual interrupt driver used by TSI Products
device=vfat.386
DEVICE=C:\WINDOWS\TRAVSOFT\TSIVID.386
LPT1AUTOASSIGN=-1
LPT2AUTOASSIGN=-1
LPT3AUTOASSIGN=-1
COM3AUTOASSIGN=-1
COM4AUTOASSIGN=-1
netmisc=ndis.386
netcard3=rasmac.386
transport=netbeui.386
netheapsize=20
InDOSPolling=FALSE
device=*blockdev
device=vsbpd.386
[standard]

[NonWindowsApp]
localtsrs=dosedit,ced

[mci]
CDAudio=mcicda.drv
Sequencer=mciseq.drv
WaveAudio=mciwave.drv

[drivers]
midimapper=midimap.drv
timer=timer.drv
; ** Wave=speaker.drv
adobekey=adobekey.drv
adobemse=adobemse.drv
Midi=sb16fm.drv
```

FIGURE 8.4: The Notepad window with the SYSTEM.INI file appearing in it.

Configuring Air Mosaic to Use the QuickTime Viewer

Actually configuring Air Mosaic to use the QuickTime viewer you've installed is quite simple.

1. Start Air Mosaic, and from the menu bar, select Options ➤ Configure. The Configuration dialog box (Figure 8.5) will appear.

2. In the Configuration dialog box, click on the Viewers button. The External Viewer Configuration dialog box will appear.

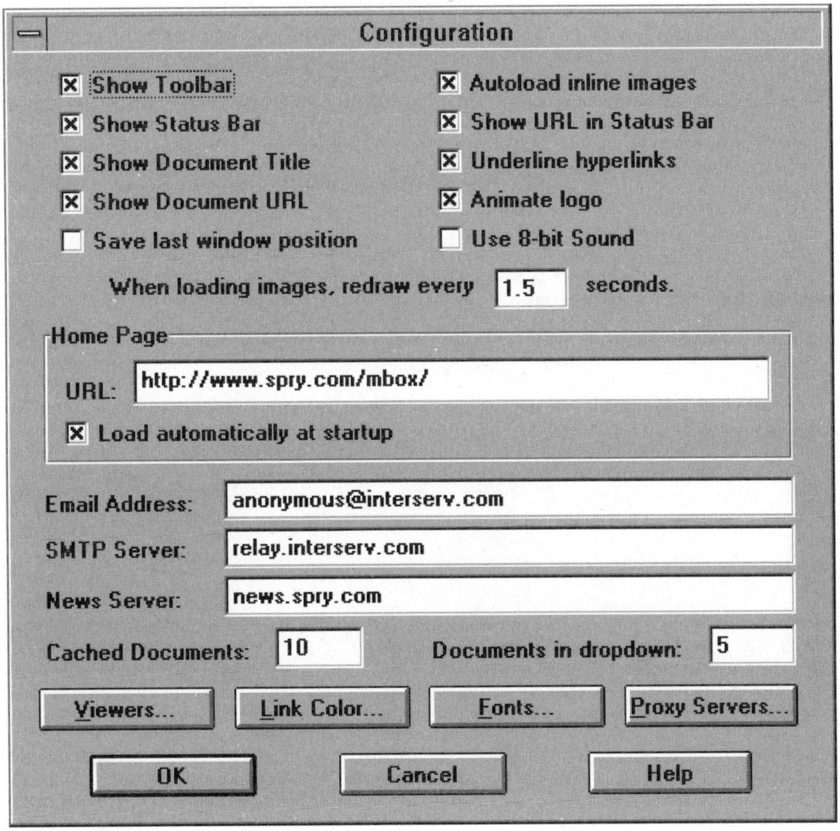

FIGURE 8.5: The Configuration dialog box

FIGURE 8.6: The External Viewer Configuration dialog box

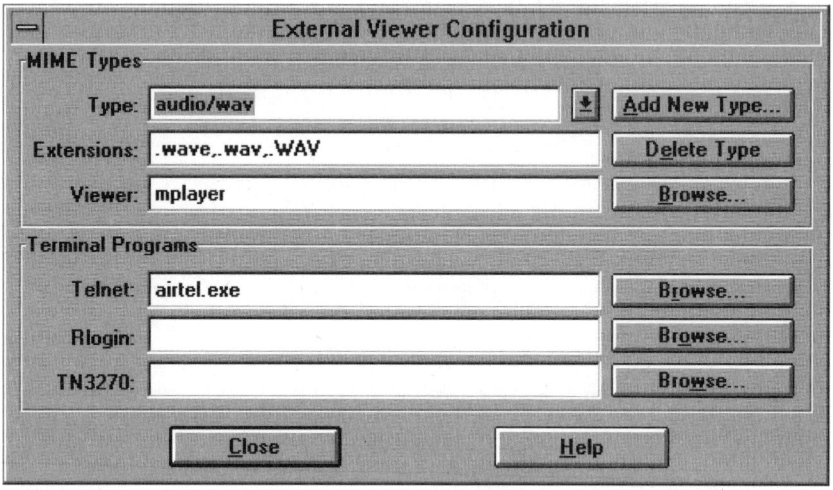

3. Pull down the Type list and select video/quicktime from the list, then type **.mov** into the Extensions box (Figure 8.6).

4. Type **mplayer** into the Viewer text box, and click on the Close button to close the External Viewer Configuration dialog box.

5. Click on OK to close the Configuration dialog box.

Now you're set—you can view QuickTime movies that are linked to Web pages simply by clicking on their links. Just remember, QuickTime movies can be many megabytes in length and take lots of time to transfer to your computer.

What's Out There?

Hollywood has premiered on the Web; you can see clips from new movies and celebrity interviews on video by sliding over to the URLs http://bvp.wdp.com/BVPM or http://www.mca.com.

Getting and Setting Up
MPEG Player

MPEG Player, the MPEG viewer we describe in this section, is highly reliable and an excellent choice for viewing MPEG video with Air Mosaic (Figure 8.7).

 To run this viewer with Windows 3.1 (as opposed to Windows 95), you must have Microsoft's Win32 extension installed. Win32 allows you to run more powerful applications under Windows 3.1; Win 32 is available for downloading free of charge. For more details about Win32 visit
`ftp://ftp.microsoft.com/peropsys/windows/kb/Q120/9/01.TXT`.

Downloading MPEG Player

Of course, before you install and configure MPEG Player, you have to download it. No problem—just follow these steps:

1. Start Air Mosaic, and from the menu bar, select File ➤ Open URL. The Open URL dialog box will appear.
2. In the Open URL dialog box's URL text box, type **ftp://ftp.ncsa.uiuc.edu/Mosaic/Windows/viewers**. Click on OK. In a few seconds the contents of the VIEWERS directory will be listed in the Air Mosaic window as a series of links.
3. Find the link labeled mpegw32h.zip and shift-click on it. The Save As dialog box will appear.
4. In the Save As dialog box's File Name text box, type **c:\mpegw32h.zip**, then click on OK.

The file will be transferred to your computer and saved. You'll see the progress of this operation in the status bar at the bottom of the window. When it's all over, you'll be ready to unzip the file and install the software. Close Air Mosaic by selecting File ➤ Exit from the menu bar.

FIGURE 8.7: A sampling of MPEG video available on the Web

Installing MPEG Player

To install MPEG Player you'll have to first create a directory into which the unzipped files will be saved, then unzip the zipped file.

1. In the Windows Program Manager's Main group, double-click on the MS-DOS icon.

MS-DOS
Prompt

The DOS prompt (C:\Windows) will appear.

2. Type **mkdir \mpeg** to create a directory called MPEG.

3. Type **cd \mpeg** to make your way into the MPEG directory you just created.

4. Now type **unzip \mpeg32h.zip** to unzip the files that make up MPEG Player. As the files are unzipped, they'll be listed along with some details, like their sizes.

5. When all the files are unzipped, type **exit** at the DOS prompt to get back to the Windows Program Manager.

There. The files are unzipped and stored in the MPEG directory. You're all set to run MPEG Player's setup (installation) program.

6. From the Windows Program Manager's menu bar, select File ➤ Run. The Run dialog box will appear.

7. In the Run dialog box's Command Line text box, type **c:\mpeg\setup.** Click on the OK button. The MPEG Player Setup window will appear (Figure 8.8).

8. In the MPEG Player Setup window you'll encounter some information about the MPEG viewer program. Read it, then click on the Continue button to continue installation. The setup program will copy a number of files from \MPEG into the WINDOWS\SYSTEM directory, and then a dialog box will appear asking where the program should install the rest of the MPEG Player software.

9. Accept the default location (\WIN32APP\MPEGPLAY) by clicking on the Continue button.

MPEG Player Setup

The setup program will install the MPEG Player in the following directory.

Path: C:\WIN32APP\MPEGPLAY

[Continue] [Back] [Exit] [Help]

Files will be copied \MPEG into the \WIN32APP\MPEGPLAY directory, and a dialog box will appear, saying everything is done.

MPEG Player Setup Exit

Setup Succeeded!

[OK]

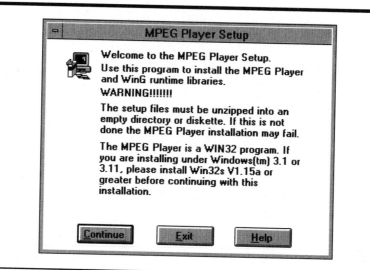

FIGURE 8.8: Read through the MPEG Player Setup window.

 You may (and you should) delete the \MPEG directory and its contents after you've successfully installed MPEG Player.

10. Click on OK and the Program Manager will reappear.

Now let's set up Air Mosaic so it will automatically call upon the MPEG Player you've installed whenever it encounters MPEG video files.

Configuring Air Mosaic to Use the MPEG Player

Configuring Air Mosaic to use the MPEG Player you've installed is as easy as pie.

1. Start Air Mosaic and select Options ➤ Configuration from the menu bar. The Configuration dialog box will appear.

2. Click on the Viewers button at the bottom of the Configuration dialog box. The External Viewer Configuration dialog box will appear.

3. Pull down the Type list and select video/mpeg. Notice as you do this that the information contained in the Extensions and Viewer boxes changes to reflect the extensions and viewer that handle MPEG video (Figure 8.9).

4. In the Viewer text box, type **c:\win32app\mpegplay\mpegply.exe**.

5. Click on the Close button. The Configuration dialog box will reappear.

6. Click on the OK button.

Now you can view MPEG video that is linked to Web pages simply by clicking on a link. Remember that MPEG video, like QuickTime movies, can be many megabytes in length and take lots of time to transfer to your computer.

What's Out There?

The MPEG movie archive is a collection of clips available for your viewing enjoyment at the URL http://peace.wit.com/surrealism/movies.

External Viewer Configuration

MIME Types

Type: video/mpeg   [Add New Type...]

Extensions: .mpeg,.mpe,.mpg   [Delete Type]

Viewer: [   ]   [Browse...]

Terminal Programs

Telnet: airtel.exe   [Browse...]

Rlogin: [   ]   [Browse...]

TN3270: [   ]   [Browse...]

[Close]   [Help]

FIGURE 8.9: The information in the Extensions and Viewer boxes will reflect the extensions and viewer that handle MPEG video.

Sound and Air Mosaic

Sun Audio (with the extension .AU) is the most common format for sound you'll find on the Net. You'll also find Microsoft Windows sound files (.WAV) and Macintosh sound files (.SND) scattered around. You can play any of these with the sound player WHAM, which you can get from the Net itself.

 Some sound cards come with their own sound-playing software. Check your sound card's documentation to find out if the software that came with it lets you play the file formats mentioned. If this is the case, you may not need to install WHAM.

Acrobat: The Quality of a Printed Page

Adobe Acrobat is a product that allows electronic documents to use many of the elements that appear in documents printed on paper: publishers of online documents using Acrobat get to fiddle around with fonts, point-size, formatting, and graphics (even wrap-around graphics) in ways usually unheard of on the Web. You can use the Acrobat Reader—a freely available program that can display Adobe Acrobat files on your computer—as an external viewer for Air Mosaic, which means you can view Acrobat files from within Air Mosaic. Adobe has created a Web page containing all types of information about Acrobat; to find out more, vault on over to http://www.adobe.com/Acrobat. You can also fairly well somersault through installing Acrobat Reader as an external viewer for Air Mosaic by following the routine outlined at http://www.adobe.com/Acrobat/SpryAIR.html.

Of course, once you've gone through the hoops of installing Acrobat Reader as an external viewer, you'll want to look at some pages that include Acrobat documents. Adobe maintains a list of such sites at the URL http://www.adobe.com/Acrobat/PDFsites.html.

One of the best uses of Acrobat on the Net is a complete set of IRS tax forms available at the URL http://www.ustreas.gov/treasury/bureaus/irs/irs.html.

To play sound on your PC, you'll need a sound card (the Sound Blaster is good), along with the proper Windows drivers. In this section we're going to assume that you have a sound-ready PC already equipped and configured.

Downloading WHAM

To use WHAM, you must first get it. Here's how to do that:

1. Start Air Mosaic, and select File ➤ Open URL from the menu bar. The Open URL dialog box will appear.

2. In the Open URL dialog box's URL text box type **ftp://ftp.ncsa.uiuc.edu/Mosaic/Windows/viewers**. Click on OK. In a few seconds, the contents of NCSA's FTP server's MOSAIC/WINDOWS/VIEWER directory will be listed in a Web page as a series of links.

3. Use the scroll bars to scroll down the list until you see the link labeled wham131.zip. This is the zipped up file you want.

4. Shift-click on wham131.zip. The Save As dialog box will appear, as shown on following page.

5. In the Save As dialog box's File Name text box, type **c:\wham131.zip**. Click on the OK button.

The zipped WHAM file will be transferred to your machine. As this happens, you can watch the progress taking place in the status bar along the bottom of the Air Mosaic window. When it's all over, quit Air Mosaic by selecting File ➤ Exit from the menu bar.

Installing WHAM

To install WHAM, the sound player, you'll unzip the files into an existing subdirectory of the Air Mosaic directory.

1. In the Windows Program Manager's Main group, double-click on the MS-DOS icon. The DOS prompt (C:\WINDOWS) will appear.

2. At the DOS prompt, type **cd \airmos\bin**.

3. Now (at the DOS prompt C:\AIRMOS\BIN) type **unzip \wham131.zip** to unzip the file. As this happens, the files that are being unzipped will be listed, along with some details, like the sizes of the files.

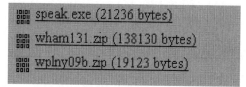

4. When it's all over, at the DOS prompt, type **exit** to return to Windows.

Now we must set up Air Mosaic so it will automatically call upon WHAM whenever it encounters AU, WAV, or SND sound files.

Configuring Air Mosaic to Use WHAM

Configuring Air Mosaic to use WHAM is no big deal. Just follow these steps:

1. Start Air Mosaic and select Options ➤ Configuration from the menu bar. The Configuration dialog box will appear.

2. Click on the Viewers button (near the bottom of the Configuration dialog box). The External Viewer Configuration dialog box (shown in Figure 8.6) will appear.

3. In the External Viewer Configuration dialog box's Type pull-down list, select audio/basic.

4. In the Viewer text box, type **wham.exe.**

5. Click on the Close button to close the External Viewer Configuration window. The Configuration dialog box will reappear.

6. Click on the OK button to close the Configuration dialog box.

Now, whenever you click on a link to go to a sound file, Air Mosaic will automatically call upon WHAM to play the sound.

What's Out There?

For a quick intro to what's happening in sound (read: *music*) on the Web, drop by the Internet Underground Music Archive (IUMA). IUMA includes digitized sound from many bands at the URL `http://www.iuma.com`.

You're All Set

So—you're a master Web navigator and burgeoning Web publisher after reading the earlier chapters in this book, and now you know how to get and use viewers to augment your Air Mosaic experience. You're ready to proceed full steam ahead into your World Wide Web travels using Air Mosaic.

Bon voyage!

Appendix

Installing
and Setting Up
the Software

Installing most Mosaics is a time-consuming process involving setting up an Internet service provider account, getting Mosaic, getting SLIP/PPP connecting software, making them both work on your machine, and so on. Spry Mosaic, the software that comes with this book, takes care of everything for you—it comes with Internet service and all the software you need, and installing it is a simple matter that takes just minutes. Basically it's a matter of popping in the disk that comes with this book and answering a few questions on screen. (There are a few things to know, however—that's why we're including this appendix.)

Spry Mosaic is the functional equivalent of Spry's Mosaic in a Box, which is sold through retail outlets. Don't worry if you see references to Mosaic in a Box in the illustrations in this book or on your screen—you have the correct software, providing you with all the functionality of Spry's Mosaic in a Box containing Air Mosaic.

What's on the Disk

On the disk that comes with this book you'll find Spry Mosaic, a software package that includes:

◆ Air Mosaic, a popular, enhanced form of the easy-to-use Web browser, Mosaic

◆ Specialized Internet access service software designed to work with CompuServe's network

◆ SLIP/PPP software that is preconfigured to work with Air Mosaic and the special CompuServe Internet access service

The best part is: these products are all preconfigured to work together so smoothly you won't even know they're there. All you'll ever see on your screen is Air Mosaic, working like a charm.

To get them going, you'll have to install the software from the disk to your hard disk. Along the way, by answering a few simple questions, you'll be telling the software a thing or two about your machine and setting up a special account with CompuServe so you can run Air Mosaic.

 The account you'll be setting up with CompuServe is specially designed to give you access to the Internet's World Wide Web via Air Mosaic—it is not an account that allows access to the CompuServe Information Service, and it cannot be used with other forms of Mosaic, or any other Web browsers.

What You Need

To use the software that comes with this book, you'll need Microsoft Windows version 3.1 or 95 and a fast modem. To be more specific, you should have at least the following:

◆ A 386 or greater CPU

◆ 4MB or more of RAM

◆ 4MB of free hard-disk space

◆ A 9600 bps (baud) or faster modem

 You absolutely must have a 9600 bps (baud) or faster modem in order to use this software. A slower modem cannot transfer data between your computer and the Internet fast enough to make a graphical Internet application like Spry's Air Mosaic worthwhile or even workable.

Installing the Software

Like we said, installing the software that comes with this book is a very simple matter. Everything happens automatically. In fact, it's more complicated to describe this installation than to just run it, so you can go ahead and install without reading this material if you want to do so.

Installing the software involves two parts—first the setup program will copy all the files to your hard disk, then the registration program will walk you through registering for your specialized CompuServe account.

 For answers to your questions about installing and using the software, call Spry's Technical Support department at (206)447-0958 Monday through Friday between the hours of 8 a.m. and 5 p.m. (Pacific standard time). For answers to your questions about billing, call Spry at (800)777-9638, also during business hours.

Running the Setup

This is no big deal. To run the setup:

1. Place the disk that comes with this book in your disk drive. (We'll assume that's drive A:; if it's drive B: on your machine, just replace the A: with a B: in these instructions.)
2. From the Windows Program Manager's menu bar, select File ➤ Run. The Run dialog box will appear.
3. In the Run dialog box's Command Line text box, type **a:setup**. Click OK. The Run dialog box will close, and, in a few seconds, a dialog box will appear asking you to specify a destination directory (the location to which you'd like to install the software) as shown at the top of the following page.

Mosaic In A Box

❓ Please enter the destination directory.

C:\SPRY

[OK]   [Cancel]

---

4. In the destination directory window you can (and you should) just click on the OK button to accept the default drive and directory, C:\SPRY, as the destination.

The setup program will describe its progress to you as it copies files to your local computer. This won't take long. Once all of the files are copied to your computer, a dialog box will appear informing you that the setup program is creating a number of *configuration* (setup) files in your Windows directory. Again, this won't take long; you can sit back and relax for a few moments. Note, however, that these files are needed for the software to function, so you should click on OK anytime you are asked to, to allow the files to be created.

5. When the setup program is finished getting the stuff it needs installed to your computer, the dialog box shown here will appear.

Quick Connection Checklist

You are about to set up your Mosaic In A Box software for connecting to the Internet.

Before connecting, please make sure that:

- You have a 9600 baud or faster modem
- Your modem is connected to a working telephone line
- If you have an external modem, it is turned on

Once connected, the software will establish an account with SPRY. Then you can start exploring!

[OK]   [Cancel]

Click on the OK button and the registration program will start running.

The registration program will register your copy of the software with its manufacturer, Spry, and set up your specialized CompuServe account for Internet access. In the next section of this appendix, we'll go over registering your copy of the software.

Getting Registered

When the program files are finished copying to your hard disk, the setup program will start the registration program. This baby gets you registered and sets you up with your specialized CompuServe account; it also takes advantage of the opportunity to find out from you a few things about your computer that the software needs to know in order to function.

When the program gets rolling, it creates an Air Mosaic group window that contains a bunch of icons, just like most other Windows-type programs. One of those icons is labeled Auto Registration. If you have some reason to stop the registration process (can't find your credit card?) you can start it up again at any time by double-clicking on the Auto Registration icon.

1. The first thing you'll see when the registration program is running is the Introduction window. Click on its OK button to get started. The Communications Port Setup dialog box will appear.

Communications Port Setup

Basic Settings

Port: ● COM1   ○ COM2   Speed: 19200

○ COM3   ○ COM4

Port Status: Available   Base-Addr: 3F8

OK

Cancel

Help

Advanced >>

2. In the Communications Port Setup dialog box you must tell the program about the way your modem is attached to your computer.

◆ First, specify which COM port your modem is attached to by clicking on the appropriate button. (Hint: it's usually COM2. If you get done, fire up Air Mosaic, and find that COM2 was wrong, go back to this point and try COM1, and like that. External modems are usually COM1 or COM2; internal modems are usually COM3 or COM4, but can be COM1 or 2 occasionally.)

◆ Second, select the speed at which your modem operates from the Speed drop-down list. (If you have a 14000 bps (baud) modem you should pick 19200, and if you have a 28800 bps (baud) modem you should select 38400.)

You can specify more advanced features about your connection by clicking on the Communications Port Setup window's Advance button. This will expand the dialog box to include options for specifying the Data Bits, Parity, Step Bits, and Flow Control to use when talking to CompuServe. You should not need to modify these settings, but if you're a tinkerer well versed in the ways of modems, you do have this option.

Once you have specified your modem's COM port and speed, click on the OK button to continue. The Communications Port Setup window will close, and the Modem Setup dialog box will appear.

3. In the Modem Setup dialog box you have to select the *type* of modem you're using.

Modem Setup		
Basic Settings		**OK**
Modem Type: Hayes	±	**Cancel**
		Help
Phone Line Type: ⦿ Tone ○ Pulse		**Advanced >>**

◆ Pull down the Modem Type drop-down list and select the name of your modem by clicking on it. If your modem is not included in the list of supported modems, select Hayes. Most modems *emulate* (act like) Hayes modems, so that's a pretty safe pick.

◆ The Tone radio button should be selected near the bottom of the dialog box to tell the software to use tone dialing. (This is true unless you still have a rotary phone line, in which case you should select the Pulse radio button and ask yourself why you and/or your phone company haven't moved on in life.)

 Selecting the Advanced button in the Modem Setup dialog box will expand the window to include options to control Auto Baud, Hangup Method, and CTS Control. Again, you should not need to modify any of these options, but they're there if you know what you're doing and feel the need to tinker.

Having told all there is to tell about your modem, select the OK button to continue. The Modem Setup dialog box will close and the Dial Modifier dialog box will appear.

The Dial Modifier dialog box allows you to add any necessary numbers that the software may have to dial before or after each phone call it makes—for example, if you are using an office phone system that requires you to dial 9 before getting an outside line, you can set that up to happen automatically using this dialog box. You can also enter the appropriate code for disabling Call Waiting if you have that feature on your phone line. (Ask your phone company for the correct code.)

4. In the Dial Modifier dialog box's Before and After text boxes, type any numbers that must be dialed before or after the phone number that gets you Internet access. Once you are done entering those numbers, click on the OK button to continue. The Dial Modifier dialog box will close, and the Software Registration dialog box will appear.

5. In the Software Registration dialog box (Figure A.1) enter your name, mailing address, and phone number where you are asked to do so. Then click on the Register button to continue. The Software Registration dialog box will close and a dialog box will appear asking you to confirm the information you just entered.

6. In the confirmation dialog box, click on the Continue button if the information you entered is correct, or on the Go Back button if you

wish to go back to step 4 and make changes before continuing. When you do click on the Continue button, an informational dialog box will appear. Read this stuff before you move on.

7. Click on OK to continue. The Internet Access Phonebook dialog box will appear.

8. In the Internet Access Phonebook window (Figure A.2) select your country, area code, and city, from the drop-down lists. This will help the registration program narrow the possibilities and present to you a short list of the most locally available phone numbers for your machine to call to get hooked up to Internet service. Those numbers will appear in the list labeled *Choose phone number (baud rate).* Just select from that drop-down list the nearest Internet access phone number to you.

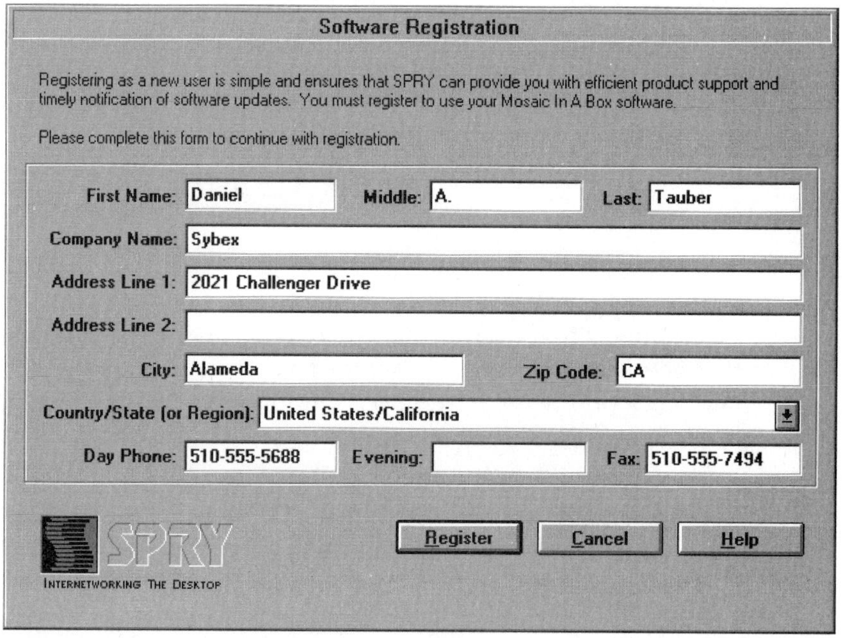

FIGURE A.1: In the Software Registration dialog box, enter your name, mailing address, and phone number. This information will be used to set up your Internet account with CompuServe.

The beauty of the specialized CompuServe account you're getting is not just skin deep—sure it's nice to have such a smooth connection and interface to use, but the really great thing is that CompuServe provides over 400 local Internet access numbers from which you can choose (most providers can boast only about 100). If you live anywhere near a reasonably sized urban area, you should find a number you can use on the drop-down list. If you live far from the madding city, you may have to pay some kind of long-distance charges, but that's life, for now.

Internet Access Phonebook

Choose the country:
United States

Choose the area code (or city code):
510

Choose the city:
Oakland, CA

Choose the phone number (baudrate):
251-8304 (9600,14400)

☐ Use long distance dialing prefix:

[OK] [Cancel] [Help] [Dial Modifiers...]

FIGURE A.2: The Internet Access Phonebook is where you pick the phone number the software will use to connect to the Internet.

If you find that the number you select in the list labeled *Choose phone number (baud rate)* is outside of your local area code, select *Use long distance dialing prefix* and be sure that the correct prefix is entered into the text box. (In most cases, the prefix should be a 1 followed by the area code to which you are calling.) Once you have selected the phone number, click on the OK button to continue. Yet another informational dialog box will appear, this time containing some pricing information.

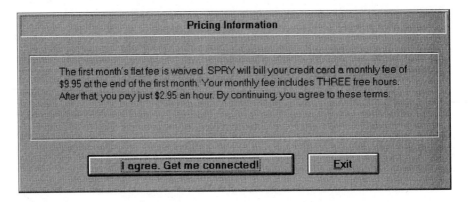

Pricing Information

The first month's flat fee is waived. SPRY will bill your credit card a monthly fee of $9.95 at the end of the first month. Your monthly fee includes THREE free hours. After that, you pay just $2.95 an hour. By continuing, you agree to these terms.

[I agree. Get me connected!]   [Exit]

9. Read the pricing information—it's important. Then click on the *I agree. Get me connected!* button. The Account Billing Information dialog box will appear.

10. In the Account Billing Information window shown in Figure A.3 you'll specify how you will be billed for your Internet account, giving the appropriate information so this can happen. You can choose to have charges billed to your Visa, Mastercard, or American Express account. You'll also have to provide your account number, expiration month and year, name as it appears on the card, and your mother's maiden name. When you've completed this information, click on the Register button.

Some people worry about their credit card data being transmitted over the Internet. Not to worry here—your credit information in this case is transmitted via a direct phone number rather than over the Internet. (Your Internet connection starts up after registration.) There is no likelihood of any kind of security breach in this case.

Account Billing Information

Credit Application Form:

In order to create and administer your Internet account, you must provide a valid credit card to be billed for connection services. This transaction occurs over a private network.

Credit Card Type: ⊙ VISA   ○ Master Card   ○ American Express

Account Number: `4128 xxx xxx xxx`   Expiration Month: `12` ⬇   Year: `97` ⬇

Name as it appears on Card: `Daniel A. Tauber`

Mother's Maiden Name: `Mom`

[<u>R</u>egister]   [<u>C</u>ancel]   [<u>H</u>elp]

FIGURE A.3: The Account Billing Information window

A dialog box will appear asking you to confirm the information you just gave. Click Continue to move on, or select Go Back to go back to the Account Billing Information dialog box and correct your entries before moving on. The registration program will verify your credit information, and as it does so a dialog box will appear on screen keeping you apprised of its activity. This will take a few minutes, usually no more.

11. Now a dialog box will appear asking for your e-mail address. If you have an e-mail address, enter it here. If you don't have an e-mail address, you can accept the default that's suggested, `anonymous@ interserv.com`. Click on OK when you're done in either case.

Outgoing Mail Setup

Mosaic In A Box has the ability to send (but not retrieve) e-mail.

All Mosaic In A Box users have a default send-only e-mail name which is "anonymous@interserv.com". If you have an existing e-mail name, please enter it below.

Specify the e-mail name to use for sending mail:

`anonymous@interserv.com`

[<u>O</u>K]   [<u>H</u>elp]

E-mail is not a primary feature of Air Mosaic—yet e-mail travels via the Web all the time. Lots of Web pages have links to people's e-mail addresses; thus, Air Mosaic allows you to send e-mail but does not provide you with an e-mail address for receiving. If you don't have an e-mail address, your incoming e-mail will go into the ethers in the form of a "dead letter" e-mail address otherwise known as anonymous@interserv.com.

12. When everything's in order, yet another dialog box will appear, this time containing important information about your account. Figure A.4 is an example. Jot down this important information and keep it in a safe place; it's a pain if something goes wrong down the road and you phone up tech support and don't have these numbers.

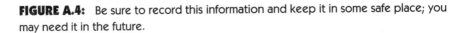

Serial # : MBX100RTL-2F42741C332A

Congratulations! You have successfully registered your software with SPRY and created an Internet access account. You are now ready to connect to the World Wide Web with Mosaic In A Box. Please record the following account information for your records.

Host name: MBOX

User ID: ISV0000000

Additional Information:

SPRY would like to welcome you to the World Wide Web! Happy Cruising!

Choose "Start Mosaic" if you would like to connect to the Internet now.

Start Mosaic   Exit

FIGURE A.4: Be sure to record this information and keep it in some safe place; you may need it in the future.

That's all there is to it—you're signed up and ready to go. A final dialog box appears giving you two options:

◆ You can click on *Start Mosaic* to start using Air Mosaic right away.

◆ You can click on *Exit* to go to the Windows Program Manager.

You can do whichever you like; note, however, that when you next visit the Windows Program Manager you'll find that Air Mosaic has its own group window, containing a bunch of icons related to the software package's various parts.

Looking at the Group Window

Now that you are finished installing the software, you should have a new group in the Window's Program Manager. The group includes the following icons:

Double-Click on This	To Start
Air Mosaic	Air Mosaic, the Web browser included in Spry Mosaic
ImageView	Image View, an image viewer used by Air Mosaic to display images in GIF and JPEG format
Internet Access Phonebook	Internet Access Phonebook, with which you can specify or change the phone number Air Mosaic should dial to reach the CompuServe network
Connection Manager	Connection Manager, the program that dials out to CompuServe's network

Double-Click on This	To Start
 Auto Registration	Auto Registration, the program that registers your copy of the software and creates your Internet account
 Mosaic Documentation	Mosaic Documentation, the documentation provided by Spry, the product's manufacturer

 With the software package installed on your computer, the only one of these programs you will need to use is Air Mosaic—it will automatically start up the other programs as they are needed. You may at times want to change something, like your Internet access phone number, in which case you can use Internet Access Phonebook. You also may want to refer occasionally to Mosaic Documentation for more detailed information about the software package.

Getting Connected and Disconnected

Because you have an integrated package including Air Mosaic, the connecting software, and a specialized CompuServe connection to the Internet, you'll never need to go through the gyrations usually involved in starting up most Mosaics and getting connected.

The Connection Manager Makes Getting Connected as Smooth as Glass

When you double-click on the Air Mosaic icon, the program will start Air Mosaic, make all the necessary connections using the Connection Manager, and get you going. This all happens behind the scenes, but the program tells you what it's up to through dialog boxes like the ones shown in Figure A.5—that's just so you'll know something's happening in the moments it takes to get connected.

Getting Disconnected Is Just as Easy

You can disconnect from the Internet just as easily, by double-clicking on the Close box in the upper-left corner of the Air Mosaic window. This will close the program. When the Connection Manager realizes that none of the programs you are using require Internet access, it will also disconnect you from the Internet. Before it does so, however, a dialog box will pop up *asking* if you want to disconnect.

You can do nothing, in which case the Connection Manager will end your connection when the timer finishes counting down, or you can click on the Hangup button to end the connection yourself. (To *stay* connected, click on Continue.)

If while you're connected you don't do anything in particular using Internet access for a period of 10 minutes, the Connection Manager will notice your inactivity and the dialog box asking if you want to disconnect will appear. If you do nothing, you'll be disconnected. (A countdown timer in the dialog box tells you how much longer you can dawdle before being disconnected.) If you click on Continue, your connection will be restored.

You can also disconnect from the Internet by selecting Modem ➤ Hangup in the Connection Manager menu bar or by selecting Hangup from the Connection Manager's system menu.

Now Get Surfing...

Now you're all set up with Spry Mosaic, complete with Air Mosaic and a specialized CompuServe Internet account—you also know how to get on and off the Internet. You're as ready as can be to surf the Net using Air Mosaic and the World Wide Web. Turn to the beginning of this book to find out how to get going in your cyberspace travels with Air Mosaic.

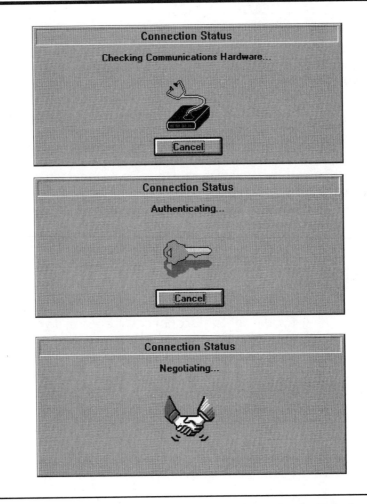

FIGURE A.5: Dialog boxes like these will tell you you're getting connected—you don't have to do anything in these moments, all the connections are made automatically.

anchors Links, from the other side of the picture—*anchor* is HTML-lingo for a text or image link to any other document.

anonymous FTP A *File Transfer Protocol* that lets *anyone* (regardless of whether he or she has a user name or password) transfer files from the server machine to his or her own.

application A computer program designed to specialize in a specific set of tasks. Word and WordPerfect are word processing applications; Excel and Quattro Pro are spreadsheet applications.

Archie A system that lets you search for files on the Internet that can be downloaded by anonymous FTP.

ARPAnet A now-defunct experimental network of the 1970s on which the theories and systems that became today's Internet were tested. AR-PAnet is short for *Advanced Research Project Agency net.*

article A message posted to Usenet and readable with a newsreader.

ASCII The acronym for *American Standard Code for Information Interchange;* a basic text format most computers can read.

authentication A security feature, authentication lets users have access to information if they can provide a user name and password that the security system recognizes.

backbone One of the high-speed networks that form the "backbone" or core of the Internet.

bandwidth The amount of data that can be sent through a communications channel such as a network or a modem.

baud A measurement of the speed at which signals are sent by a modem (more precisely, a measurement of the number of changes per second that occur during transmission). A baud rate of 2400, for example, indicates that 2400 signal changes occur in one second. Baud rate is often confused with *bps* (bits per second), which is defined below.

BBS An online *bulletin board system;* an electronic place provided by kind strangers or misguided entrepreneurs for people with like interests to post (make public) messages in an ongoing conversation, and to upload and download software and files.

binary transfer A transfer of data between computers in which binary data is preserved; often the best type of transfer for software and graphic images.

bitmap An electronic file that represents an image with a collection of bits. (A bit is smaller than a byte.)

bounced message A message that has been returned is known as one that has *bounced.* Usually this happens because the address was incorrect.

bps A measurement—*bits per second*—of the speed at which data is transferred between modems. Higher bps rates indicate faster transfer.

browser Software that enables the user to look at, interact with, and generally "browse" files on the Internet.

BTW Electronic shorthand for *by the way.*

bye A log-off command that means essentially "quit" or "exit."

cd A shorthand version of the commonly used command *change directory.*

cdup A shorthand version of the command *change directory up*, which is used at FTP sites to go from a subdirectory up to its parent directory.

CERN *The Conseil Européen pour la Recherche Nucleaire*—the European particle physics laboratory that was the birthplace of the World Wide Web.

client A computer that *receives;* the computer that connects to a *server.* *See* server.

compressed   (a)A term used to describe data that has been *shrunk* or "zipped." This process, performed by utility programs like PKZip, LHArc, and Zip, makes it possible to conserve storage space and to transfer files more quickly. (b) A process of shrinking motion picture files by leaving out some frames, retaining only as many as are necessary to create the perception of action. QuickTime and MPEG are examples of the use of this process.

CWIS   A menu-based system at a university that provides on-line information about the university. CWIS is short for *Campus-Wide Information System.*

dedicated   A line, server, or other piece of computer-associated equipment that has only one purpose; a *dedicated line,* for example, might be a phone line that leads *only* to your PC (or modem) and *not* also to a phone.

dial-up   A connection to a computer that is accomplished by calling on a phone line with a modem.

dir   A shorthand version of the commonly used command *directory.* If at a DOS prompt or an FTP site you type **dir** and press ⏎, you will see the contents of the current directory.

distribution   A variation on the original software, usually enhanced, that is being distributed by parties who did not develop the software but who are licensed or permitted to add to and distribute the software. This differs from a *version* in that it does not represent a generation in the development of the software. Air Mosaic is an enhanced distribution of the original Mosaic.

domain   A level in an address, as defined in the Domain Name System (see below). In the address, domains are separated from each other by a period, as in ed.sybex.com.

Domain Name system   A system for classifying computers into increasingly large groups with names; for example, in the domain name laxness.ed.sybex.com, *laxness* is a specific machine in a group named *editorial* in a company called *sybex* which is in the general category of *com*mercial.

download   To transfer files to your machine from another machine.

drive   A physical device on which you can store files. Each drive is identified by a letter (A:, B:, C:, etc.).

driver A program that tells your computer what to do with something added to your computer—a printer, mouse, sound board, etc.

e-mail The common way to refer to *electronic mail;* messages that are addressed to an individual at a computer and sent electronically.

emoticon *See* smiley.

encryption Disguising a message (by scrambling it) to prevent intruders from reading it.

FAQ Electronic shorthand for *frequently asked question.*

file transfer The transfer of a file from one computer to another over a network or via a modem.

finger A program that finds and provides information about a user who might be logged in to your network or the Internet.

firewall A security system that creates an electronic barrier protecting an organization's network and PCs from access by outsiders via the Internet.

flame A very unfriendly, often violent, written attack against someone in an electronic forum such as a newsgroup or message area. (A *flame war* occurs when both parties engage in and continue such an exchange, perhaps even inspiring others in the newsgroup or message area to take sides.)

form support To *support* is to allow for, or to be capable of using; a program that has form support is one that allows for (is capable of using) on-screen *forms,* which are on-screen versions of the types of forms you'd usually see on paper.

Free-net A network in a community providing free access to the Internet; often the Free-net includes the community's own forums and news.

freeware Programs that are distributed free of charge by those who developed them.

front end The "face" you see on a program, its *interface* is also often called its *front end*. Sometimes, one program provides a *front end* for other programs or for viewing data or files. Thus, Air Mosaic is a front end for the Internet.

FTP The acronym for *File Transfer Protocol,* a standard, agreed-upon way for electronic interaction to occur in the transferring of files from one computer to another.

FYI Electronic shorthand for *for your information.*

gateway A computer system that transfers data or messages between programs or networks that are normally incompatible.

gopher A menu-based system for finding directories on the Internet. Gopher will "go-fer" what you ask it to find.

graphical Represented by pictures or icons.

gui Short for *graphical user interface;* a gui provides a way for you to interact with your computer by pointing and clicking or otherwise manipulating pictures and icons on the screen.

hack To fiddle around "behind the scenes" in a program or system, presumably to make improvements or to find out how the thing works. (A "hacker" is actually someone who makes furniture with an axe. No kidding.)

header The information at the *head* or top of a page, as in the message header containing the To:, From:, and Time/Date information in an e-mail message.

hit A single access of an Internet resource (example: the Enterzone home page gets over 2,000 *hits* per day).

home page The first page you see when you encounter a World Wide Web resource.

host *See* server.

Hotlist In Mosaic, a list of your favorite URLs.

HTML The acronym for *HyperText Markup Language;* the language used to make ordinary text into Web documents. HTML + includes enhancements to HTML.

HTTP The acronym for *HyperText Transfer Protocol;* the agreed-upon standard way for electronic interaction to occur in the transferring of Web documents on the Internet.

hypermedia Hypertext combined with graphics, sound, and even video.

hypertext Text that includes links to other documents.

IMHO Electronic shorthand for *in my humble opinion.*

Infobahn The hip and cool term for the so-called information superhighway.

inline image A graphic *in* a Web page—a graphic that does not have to be downloaded to be viewed.

interface The "face" a program shows you, with which you interact.

Internet A global, interconnected network of networks and single computers that act as if they were networks.

IP The acronym for *Internet Protocol; see* TCP/IP.

ISOC The acronym for *Internet Society;* a group whose purpose is to support and govern the Internet.

knowbot An information-retrieval tool, still experimental but wonderfully named.

LAN The acronym for *local area network;* a lot of machines (well, at least *two*) cabled together so they can share resources like printers and software.

link A connection between Web documents, sometimes called a *hot link.*

local Your local machine is the one on your desk, the one that's nearby. Your local drive is the one on your machine. Local is the opposite of *remote.*

lurker Someone who lurks about on a newsgroup or other interactive forum without contributing anything to the talk. A silent voyeur. Many people think it best to lurk for a while before you join in, that way you'll get to know the customs and avoid social blunders.

modem The device that connects your computer to a phone line so you can make connections via the phone line to other modems, which are connected to remote machines.

Mosaic Any of a group of programs that let you browse hypertext pages on the World Wide Web.

multimedia The combination and use of *multiple types of media* (graphics, sound, video, and text) in a single document or presentation.

NCSA The acronym for *National Center for Supercomputing Applications;* a federally funded research lab run by the University of Illinois that was the birthplace of the original Mosaic.

network A lot of (or even just two) computers linked via cables or phone lines so they can share resources, such as software, printers, etc.

network administrator The person who organizes, maintains, troubleshoots, and generally watches over a network.

newsgroups Usenet message areas, each of which is focused on a particular topic.

node A machine on the Internet.

online To be ready or electronically connected.

operating system A program that controls the most basic functions of a computer.

packet Data bundled together—a packet may be thought of as similar to an envelope full of data, with some of the data contained in the envelope actually representing the address or destination information. Packets of data traverse the Internet independently of each other because IP, the internet protocol, is connectionless and orderless.

path The complete description of the location of a file on a specific machine.

ping A utility that lets you see whether a machine is working and connected to the network by sending out a packet that "pings" (or echoes back) when it encounters a specified remote machine.

point-and-click access An Internet access account that provides you with a Windows-type graphical user interface—one in which you point and click your way around the Internet. Spry's Air Mosaic and Netcom's NetCruiser are examples. *See* gui, shell account.

point of presence A phone number that gives you (presumably) local access to a specific Internet service provider. Sometimes, unfortunately, there's quite a distance from the nearest point of presence (POP) to you, in which case you may be charged long-distance fees by your phone company for the time you're online. Air Mosaic, via its Internet service provider (CompuServe) provides over 400 POPs so you're likely to find one located near you.

port   (a) One of a machine's input/output plugs. (b) A number that identifies a particular Internet server.

post   To make public, as in *posting a message*.

PPP   The acronym for *Point-to-Point protocol;* an agreed-upon way for the interaction to occur on a phone line which allows packets to be transferred along an Internet connection.

protocol   An agreed-upon way for an interaction to occur.

public domain   To be in the public domain is to be *not* copyrighted; to be available to the public at large.

real-time   The Internet term that means *live,* as in "real-time conversation" (a *chat*).

remote   Somewhere else. A *remote machine* is not near you; it is somewhere else.

robot   An information gathering tool; a program that wanders the Web gathering data and building a database of resources. Also known as a *spider* or *wanderer.*

router   A machine that transfers packets of data between networks.

RTFM   Electronic shorthand for *read the f***ing manual.*

searchable   A document that contains keywords making it easier to search for the specific information contained in the document.

server   A computer that *serves;* the computer that provides stuff to a *client. See* client.

service provider   The company or organization that provides a connection to the Internet.

shareware   Software that is made available by its developer for people to use on a trial basis and, if they like it, to continue to use in exchange for a one-time fee.

shell account   A Unix-based Internet access account—one in which you have to type Unix commands to make your way around the Internet. Portal Communications and Netcom offer shell accounts, as do some other service providers and many universities. *See* point-and-click access.

SLIP The acronym for *Serial Line Internet Protocol;* an agreed-upon way for the interaction to occur on a phone line allowing packets to be transferred along an Internet connection.

smiley Any of a *lot* of little pictures drawn with keyboard characters to indicate an emotion or to illustrate a sentence. The first one in common use was meant to indicate a smile. : -)

snail-mail What the U.S. Postal Service carries and delivers.

support To *support* is to allow for the use of; as an example, software that supports hypertext is software that allows you to view or create hypertext.

system administrator *See* network administrator.

TCP The acronym for *Transmission Control Protocol; see* TCP/IP.

TCP/IP The acronym for *Transmission Control Protocol/Internet Protocol;* the agreed-upon way machines on the Internet interact with each other by sending packets across multiple networks until they reach their destinations.

telnet An Internet program with which you can log onto another machine (with permission, of course).

time out What happens when two machines are interacting and one does not respond—the other one times out.

Unix The operating system used to develop the Internet.

upload To transfer files from your machine to another machine.

URL The acronym for *Universal Resource Locator;* an address or location of a document on the World Wide Web.

Usenet An informal, anarchistic network of machines that exchange public messages, also known as *news.* Usenet newsgroups tend to focus on specific topics.

Veronica A system, very similar to Archie, that lets you search gopher sites for menu items.

version A new form of a program, usually with new features and tools; often the version is indicated by a number tacked onto the end of the program's name.

viewer A program that lets you view (or otherwise experience) a certain type of data—for example, a viewer is necessary to view video; another viewer is necessary to "view" sound (which you don't see but rather hear).

WAIS The acronym for *Wide Area Information Service;* a system for searching by keyword for information in databases around the Internet.

Wanderer *See* robot.

Web *See* World Wide Web.

workstation (a) The physical area where you work on your computer. (b) A desktop computer, typically more powerful than a PC, running Unix.

World Wide Web On the Internet, a loose network of documents of different types, connected to each other through hypertext links embedded in the documents themselves.

Worm *See* robot.

zip, zipped *See* compressed.

Index

Note to the Reader: Throughout this index **boldfaced** page numbers indicate primary discussions of a topic. *Italicized* page numbers indicate illustrations page numbers indicate illustrations.

maps
earthquake, 114, *115*
of NASA centers, 110, *111*
viewer for, 116, *116*
Viking Orbiter, 107–108
of WWW servers, **94**, *95*
mark-up languages, 27–29, *28*,
159–163. *See also* HTML
(HyperText Markup Language)
Mars Atlas home page, **107–108**, *109*
maximum number of documents
flag in Veronica searches, 155
McBryan, Oliver, 147
medical information, **110–113**, *112*
menu bar, 55
messages
bounced, 234
e-mail. *See* e-mail
on Usenet, **72–76**, *74–76*
Metaverse home page, **129–131**, *130*
Microsoft, URL for, 24
Microsoft Windows
initialization files in, 202–204,
203–204
programs for, 196
sound files in, 212
MIDI files, 40
.mil domain, 35
mineral resources information, 114
minorities issues, 122
MIT Laboratories links, 106
MIT/LCS, 20
MIT Media Lab, 107
MIT Microwave Subnode of NASA's
Planetary Data System, 106–107
MIT SIPB home page, **104–107**, *105*
Modem ➤ Hangup command, 231
Modem Setup dialog box, 222–223,
222
modems, 238
ports for, 221–222
requirements for, 218–219
setting up, **222–223**

Mosaic, 19, **27–29**, *28*, 238. *See also*
Air Mosaic; Spry Mosaic
Mosaic Documentation icon, 230,
230
Mosaic in a Box, **19**, 54, *54*, 84, **217**
MOV files, 40, 197
movies
archives for, 211
clips from, 206
database for, **132–133**
links for, 180
viewers for, 195–196, *196*. *See also*
MPEG Player; QuickTime viewer
MPEG compression standard, 40
MPEG movie archive, 211
MPEG Player, 197, **207**, *208*
configuring, **210–211**, *211*
downloading, **207**
installing, **208–210**
MPEG Player Setup window, 209,
209–210
MS-DOS icon, 202, *202*, 208, *208*
MUDs (Multi-User Dungeons), 15
multimedia, 238
museums, Exploratorium, **103–104**,
105
music
Internet Underground Music
Archive, 170, *171*, 215
links for, 180
on Metaverse, **129–131**
Rolling Stones, **29–32**, *32*
Woodstock '94, 130–131

N

Name This Hotlist dialog box, 70, *71*
names
for domains, **33–36**, *33*, 235
for files, **63–65**
for Hotlist categories, 69–70, *71*
for Hotlist subcategories, 71
in Worm searches, 145–146

T

U

V

GET A FREE CATALOG JUST FOR EXPRESSING YOUR OPINION.

Help us improve our books and get a *FREE* full-color catalog in the bargain. Please complete this form, pull out this page and send it in today. The address is on the reverse side.

Name _____ Company _____

Address _____ City _____ State ____ Zip _____

Phone (___) _____

1. How would you rate the overall quality of this book?

❑ Excellent
❑ Very Good
❑ Good
❑ Fair
❑ Below Average
❑ Poor

2. What were the things you liked most about the book? (Check all that apply)

❑ Pace
❑ Format
❑ Writing Style
❑ Examples
❑ Table of Contents
❑ Index
❑ Price
❑ Illustrations
❑ Type Style
❑ Cover
❑ Depth of Coverage
❑ Fast Track Notes

3. What were the things you liked *least* about the book? (Check all that apply)

❑ Pace
❑ Format
❑ Writing Style
❑ Examples
❑ Table of Contents
❑ Index
❑ Price
❑ Illustrations
❑ Type Style
❑ Cover
❑ Depth of Coverage
❑ Fast Track Notes

4. Where did you buy this book?

❑ Bookstore chain
❑ Small independent bookstore
❑ Computer store
❑ Wholesale club
❑ College bookstore
❑ Technical bookstore
❑ Other _____

5. How did you decide to buy this particular book?

❑ Recommended by friend
❑ Recommended by store personnel
❑ Author's reputation
❑ Sybex's reputation
❑ Read book review in _____
❑ Other _____

6. How did you pay for this book?

❑ Used own funds
❑ Reimbursed by company
❑ Received book as a gift

7. What is your level of experience with the subject covered in this book?

❑ Beginner
❑ Intermediate
❑ Advanced

8. How long have you been using a computer?

years _____

months _____

9. Where do you most often use your computer?

❑ Home
❑ Work

❑ Both
❑ Other _____

10. What kind of computer equipment do you have? (Check all that apply)

❑ PC Compatible Desktop Computer
❑ PC Compatible Laptop Computer
❑ Apple/Mac Computer
❑ Apple/Mac Laptop Computer
❑ CD ROM
❑ Fax Modem
❑ Data Modem
❑ Scanner
❑ Sound Card
❑ Other _____

11. What other kinds of software packages do you ordinarily use?

❑ Accounting
❑ Databases
❑ Networks
❑ Apple/Mac
❑ Desktop Publishing
❑ Spreadsheets
❑ CAD
❑ Games
❑ Word Processing
❑ Communications
❑ Money Management
❑ Other _____

12. What operating systems do you ordinarily use?

❑ DOS
❑ OS/2
❑ Windows
❑ Apple/Mac
❑ Windows NT
❑ Other _____

13. On what computer-related subject(s) would you like to see more books?

_____

_____

_____

_____

14. Do you have any other comments about this book? (Please feel free to use a separate piece of paper if you need more room)

_____

_____

_____

_____

- - - - - - - - - - PLEASE FOLD, SEAL, AND MAIL TO SYBEX - - - - - - - - - -

SYBEX INC.
Department M
2021 Challenger Drive
Alameda, CA
94501

What's on the Spry Mosaic Disk?

Everything You Need to Explore the World Wide Web in Style!

With Spry Mosaic you can access and enjoy the beautiful, graphical World Wide Web instantly. You won't have to download or configure anything. On the single disk that comes with this book is a licensed copy of Spry Mosaic, which is the functional equivalent of Spry's popular *Mosaic in a Box*. This software includes:

◆ **Air Mosaic**, the best-selling Web browser that received *PC Magazine's* **"Best Products of 1994" award**

◆ **An integrated connection to the Internet** via CompuServe's specialized service that gives you:

  ◆ Local access virtually wherever you are (as long as you have a three-digit area code)

  ◆ Automatic set up—the software will set up your connection and your account in a few minutes

◆ **A friendly Windows interface**, giving you an intuitively simple and familiar way to use the Internet

Spry Mosaic is your low-cost alternative for accessing the Internet. The first month's flat fee is waived. SPRY will bill your credit card a monthly fee of $9.95 at the end of the first month. Your monthly fee includes **three** free hours. After that, you pay just $2.95 an hour.

Customer Support and Technical Support Are Provided by Spry, Inc.

For technical support, call (206) 447-0958 Monday through Friday between 8 a.m. and 5 p.m. (Pacific standard time). For billing questions, call (800) 777-9638, also during business hours.

©1995 SYBEX, Inc.

©1995 Spry, Inc.